# Seek, Not for Love

## Removing Your Barriers to Peace, Authenticity and Enlightenment

Donna Lee Humble

Edited by Erin E. Kannon
Back Cover Photo by Olive & West Photography
ISBN: 978-1-7372626-2-6

# Dedication

I don't know you any more than I know me. And so, to the extent that I know me, I do know you. And from a higher place, I do know you and me beyond the clouds that seem to obscure vision. I know the longing for peace and the desire to live and be your best. I know the pain, anguish, and heartbreak that has flattened you over and over again. I know the love and light that exists within you. Because in truth you know me, and we are, in reality, one. You have experienced exuberant joy as well as the depths of numbing grief. You have witnessed the incredible highs and fallacious lows that I've experienced too, and so I dedicate this book to you.

"I **am**, by calling, a **dealer in words**; and **words** are, of course, the most powerful drug used by mankind."

– Rudyard Kipling

My gift to you. Within this book you'll find more than words. If you focus on the spaces between the words you will see clearly the love that extends to you. May you allow yourself to receive it. If my words touch you and help you navigate back to the love that you are, my gift has been received. May the words on the coming pages become a bridge to realizing your perfect innocence and infallibility. Most importantly may the pages in this book connect you with your inner Guide and reveal to you your higher Self. I trust that love will then reflect the beauty that you realize in yourself back to all whom you encounter including me, for giving is synonymous with receiving.

Love and Light,

Donna Lee Humble

Donna Lee not only shares her very personal, painful early life journey but what she has learned and how she has bloomed along the way. We are our own hard-packed ground. We can choose to till it up, nurture ourselves and create our own fertile soil to grow.

Donna Lee shares what her experience has been in the areas of mental, physical and emotional breakthrough with a servant's heart to shine the light on your path of living in your authentic nature, with integrity and love.

May you embrace and enjoy many "ordinary moments" on your journey through this book.

Danielle Howard, CFP ®CKA®
Author, *Your Financial Revolution*

---

Navigating our way through the complexities of life can sometimes feel overwhelming. Life isn't always easy and setbacks can often throw us off course so far that we completely lose our way.

When you're ready to stop, sit, tune in, and deliberately map a new future with heart and integrity, Donna Lee Humble is a time-tested and proven-effective guide worthy of your time, energy, and investment.

She's traversed life's triumphs and tribulations, finding her way back to passion and purpose again and again. Highly recommended for those seeking an intentional practice with long-lasting results.

Evan Michael Zislis
Author, *ClutterFree Revolution: Simplify Your Stuff, Organize Your Life & Save the World*

---

*Seek, Not for Love* is the courageous account of one woman's transition from illness, addiction and suffering to a vibrant and abundant life lived with strength, ease, purpose, and peace. At times memoiresque, Donna Lee Humble shares this journey – acknowledging aspects of surrender, forgiveness, and emotional release, and the immense potential that exists when we learn to harness and trust our intuition.

Humble is a compassionate and skillful guide. She teaches that we all have the ability to identify and clear toxicities from body, mind and spirit. We can create a flow and access path that connects us to our higher Selves. With this inner-Guide as a grounding presence and anchor, we begin a more spiritual process of accessing the divine within.

*Seek, Not for Love* is a guided invitation for those interested in finding peace in "ordinary moments", those looking to release long-held toxic narrative, and those eager to lessen the burden of worry, guilt, shame and other difficult emotions that can leave us feeling stuck in unhealth and dis-ease. Humble offers a framework and inspired testimonial to begin this beautiful process.

Kendra Maruyama, NBC–HWC
www.howtobeinabody.com

# Table of Contents

# Acknowledgements

My family of origin. My beloved parents, grandparents, and siblings. My children, Jeremy and Jacinda, who survived my parenting attempts, allowed me to make living amends by becoming a better mother and friend today, and bestowed upon me huge lessons and insights when needed. It's true the old adage: our children are here to teach us. I have learned more from the two of you than you may know. My niece, Janae, and nephews, Joshua and Brian, who allow me to see their mother and my sister, Jackie, in their faces, mannerisms, and laughter. My dear sister, Pamela, who has given me loyalty in all my endeavors. I appreciate you beyond words. My husband, Dwayne. You continually encourage me, read over my work, and offer practical suggestions. Thank you, Dwayne, for also being a patient and tolerant life partner and sounding board.

How could I forget my grandchildren – each of them inspires me to be and to do my very best. Thanks to my eldest granddaughter, Jacelyn, for your ability to see the big picture and getting me unstuck in the organization of this book. Because you are so well read, your suggestions have proven most invaluable. My first grandson, Jesiah, for your amazing musical and artistic abilities and for reminding me of who we really are regardless of stature; Lexi for your laughter, athleticism, and being my tennis partner; Gage for your wise brown eyes and tender spirit mixed with lots of active play.

Thanks to Evan Zislis for decluttering my life so that I could proceed with writing this book and for sharing his best secrets and experience as an author. Thanks to Holly Gildar for keeping my ducks in a row during the writing process as well as your spectacular last-minute suggestions prior to publishing. A special thanks to Erin Kannon. Your professional integrity, intuitiveness and gentle editing created a better flow while keeping the message intact. And lastly to every colleague, client, workshop participant, and author before me who I worked with in person or through studying their books. Each of you provided proof that the concepts I am sharing really do work and that there is goodness in all of us. You lit the spark for my personal growth and belief that I had something of value to share too.

# Foreword

This book is the real, raw story of one woman's journey from pain, abuse, addiction and struggle to joy, peace, freedom and self-love. Whether your story is completely different from Donna Lee Humble's or even shares a few common threads, I believe you will find something powerful here to help you navigate your own journey and make your life more meaningful.

When I first met Donna Lee, she was a Wellness Coach-in-training through my organization, The International Association of Wellness Professionals (IAWP). Like many students in our Holistic Wellness Coach Certification, Donna Lee wanted to take her own wellness to the next level to better herself as well as to better support her clients.

What I noticed immediately about Donna Lee was her willingness to do the inner work that is required for a true transformation in wellness. While it's easy to join a training program and breeze through the reading and exercises and get your degree or certificate, the real learning comes from the personal application. When you apply what you learn to your own life, a deep personal transformation can occur and that is exactly what Donna Lee committed herself to do. She took to heart everything she was learning and applied it to her own life. I watched her transform from an extremely talented but struggling health practitioner to an empowered, thriving coach and leader.

Today Donna Lee Humble is one of the IAWP's greatest Wellness Coach success stories because of the impact she has made in the lives of the many people she has supported. People who have experienced Donna Lee's healing work and wellness coaching have resolved lifelong struggles with health challenges, anxiety, fear, stress and more. I believe this is because Donna Lee was dedicated to her own personal transformation. She truly walks her talk.

Combining her personal journey, years of training, self-development and professional experience, Donna Lee has mastered what it means to live and be truly well. In the pages ahead, you will get to experience her transformation first-hand and embark on your own journey to understanding yourself and living a life with more clarity and peace of mind.

Recently I had the chance to meet Donna Lee in person. Having known her virtually for almost a decade, we had talked many times through phone calls, virtual classes and online video conferencing. When I finally had the chance to meet Donna Lee in person, I noticed something. She was exactly the same in person as she was from all of those virtual interactions over the years - authentic, heart-felt and caring - except for one thing . . .

In person I noticed something else about her. She had a glow emanating from her presence. At first, I was taken a back and thought maybe the sunlight was entering the window a certain way. We took some photos during our time together and later looking at the photos, I noticed the glow was still there, shining around her in the photograph. I knew then that Donna Lee has such a powerful inner light that it actually shines through her and touches those she meets. I feel honored to have experienced her glow.

Through this book, you will learn of Donna Lee's thirty-year journey of struggle, self-discovery and hope. I can only guess that the glow she now shines out to others came from the commitment to her own inner journey and her dedication to turn her pain and suffering into meaning. I believe this book could help you in many ways, especially if . . .

- You've experienced pain and suffering and haven't found a way to heal it
- You want to understand yourself on a deeper, spiritual level
- You have big emotions and everything seems to affect you
- You've tried every self-help tool but feel something is still missing
- You simply want to find a way to enjoy the moments of your life

The pages ahead will ultimately guide you to a step-by-step process that Donna Lee has developed through her years of self-study, professional training and holistic health practice supporting real people to overcome their challenges.

While you may not get to meet Donna Lee in person as I did, I believe by reading this book you will experience her glow and be left with a gift just for you.

Love, Health & Success,

Suzanne Monroe

Author, *Live Well Dream Big: The Ultimate Guide to Becoming Your Best Self and Living Life On Your Own Terms*
Founder, The International Association of Wellness Professionals
iawpwellnesscoach.com

# Introduction

Is it the time we're living in? The media? The constant busyness? A time when we're filled with distraction. Distraction from the truth of who we are. Distractions that serve to keep us stuck and continually looking outside ourselves for the next quick fix.

We are living in the future, plagued with worry of what might happen, anxiety stricken, defeated, depressed, and filled with past regrets and resentments. This is not new. It is the human condition. Though it varies widely, it is played out. It has existed since the beginning of time. History reveals this very condition repeatedly. The egoic delusion: war, violence, suffering, dissatisfaction, yearning, hunger, and death have continued since the birth of time.

Welcome to the realm of ego. We are running from ourselves. It only changes when we wake up. Sometimes a series of bad luck brings this on, though more often we just get fed up with our lives. We hit the wall so to speak. In my case it wasn't external circumstances that woke me up. I just felt dead inside. It doesn't matter how we arrive. It only matters that we do. Somehow, we become ready. Ready to stop looking outside of ourselves for the answers. We become willing to look within.

We also become unwilling to repeat history. The world we live in is constantly changing, but there is an ancient memory that transcends the world of chaos. This place is as close as your breath and heartbeat. This place is within you. A place of certainty, a knowing. A place of complete security, transcending beauty, ineffable peace, and eternal love. A place where perfect peace never changes.

If a way through does not show up in this crucial, catalytic moment when you become ready, you will most likely recede back into the old habits that kept you stuck. You lose the opportunity to wake up and change the course of your life. You are then in danger of falling back asleep. You are beyond reason, compelled to continue striving and driving for goals that never satisfy. The loop of blinding distractions may look like this: a quick fix in the periphery, in the name of comfort and fun. You use sugar, caffeine, mind-altering substances, shopping, media, food, the latest fad diet, trendy clothing, exercise or relationship drama to get your fix. It may be that you have become consumed with political, economic, or ecological issues. You can easily remain in this quiet or not so quiet dissatisfaction for years or, worse, your entire existence on earth.

There is another way. Most of us agree that we are not the body we inhabit. We are spiritual beings. We are on earth to wake up. It is not by running away from all that brings us discomfort and pain. We evolve by diving into our discontent and dissatisfaction. At this point, you may wonder if I'm crazy or a bit on the masochistic side. Perhaps, but the purpose of the words in this book are meant to act as a guide, a proven method for utilizing your barriers, or personal distractions, to bring you back to the peace that has always been within.

Maybe it is the times. I have come across droves of people who want more. Who want something they call enlightenment, inner peace or happiness. They want freedom from the numbing emptiness that permeates their existence. The plethora of quick fixes are no longer enough. They have become bored and weary. Or worse, by trying to outrun their discontent they may have encountered life threatening illness or addictive behaviors. The bottom line is their own ways no longer work. Something is missing.

"Seek not to **change** the **world**, but choose to **change** your **mind** about the world."

- *A Course in Miracles*

If you're lucky, you've reached a point of alacrity. It may seem like you've spent lifetimes getting nowhere. You may feel dead inside, as I once did. To continue this way is no longer acceptable. You will succeed when and if you begin to realize that there has got to be another way. Deep down you know there is a purpose for your existence. It may be faint, but you hear the call. You are desperate for a change in mind. You may be feeling lost, exhausted, dissatisfied, empty. For you, this book may act as a bridge.

I am *not* offering a quick fix. I am extending proven life transforming solutions. Can you relate to some or all of the following statements?

> You catch yourself overdoing, over-giving and overthinking.
>
> You are fatigued from negative thinking.
>
> You are swimming in a sea of emotional overwhelm.
>
> You find yourself eating simply to escape.
>
> You spend hours in the vitamin aisle trying to cure the sick and tired that plague you.
>
> You jump into the short-lived, quick fixes of TV, social media, food and alcohol.

With the wisdom revealed in the coming pages, you will discover a new way –

> How to access your higher Self.
>
> You will uncover what is blocking your joy and correct imbalance in all areas of your life.
>
> You will learn the formula for authentic peace.

You will begin to easily come back to center, ending the cycle of negative thinking and looking for peace and joy outside of yourself.

Most importantly – you will allow creativity to flow, tap into real empowerment and gain a depth of spiritual resilience. You are no longer fearing the worst or waiting for something to go wrong, but are able to navigate life's perceived ups and downs with grace and gratitude.

You will be able to –

Come back to your inner emotionally calm center even while in mid conversation.

Put an end to the endless cycle of negative thinking and incessant mind chatter and self-doubt that keeps you up at night.

Embrace and correct imbalance in all areas of your life with confidence.

Finally live with certain purpose and peace.

Rediscover your authentic higher Self.

*A Course in Miracles* puts it this way:

"Your purpose is to see the world through your own holiness. Thus, are you and the World blessed together."

My goal in this book is to offer you tools to connect more readily to these higher concepts so you need not exist, stuck in endless misery, like I did. When these steps began revealing themselves to me, I was an unhealthy health practitioner, constantly sick with one ailment after another, addicted to sugar, dieting, drama, and worry, in a rocky marriage, and suffered from insomnia. I burdened myself with having to do for everyone and fix everything, especially what was clearly out of my control.

Through my soul searing trauma, I discovered not a way out but a way through! The reason I believe I was led to write this book was to save you years of misery. I recall searching frantically for support and coming up emptyhanded time and time again. A myriad of dead-ends and band-aid approaches. I want you to know there is another way of perceiving our existence on earth.

A traumatic childhood segued into early marriage and motherhood, addictive tendencies, and mental illness. Filled with unstable thinking met with many mistakes raising children. Multiple divorces were followed by mysterious illnesses. Then I climbed out the hard way. Fortunately, on my path of hard knocks, I gathered one tool after another that really worked. A long arduous thirty years. Finally, I miraculously emerged from it all with a five-step formula for living and growing that works no matter what. To my delight, I extend these tools to you to apply to your life now, raising your vibration and sense of fulfillment.

The good news: a new way is as close as your willingness to embrace all that shows up in the present moment. In reality, you are already there. You are already enlightened. You are the love you've been seeking. Each person, past or present, can arrive at this place of perfect peace in an instant.

Those who hear the call move toward slowing down. They begin to step out of time with the ego and enter the flow of the Divine. They courageously embrace the good, the bad, and the ugly that unfolds before them. They dive in and discover their wholeness. The ego nature dissolves which is, in my experience, the biggest barrier to inner peace and lasting joy. The ego is really nothing. What is nothing can become something if we resist it, and ego thoughts, if allowed, control every aspect of this world. [Note: In this book, ego may be noted as the small mind, and is synonymous with the lowercase self, the voice in our head. *A Course in Miracles* defines it as "A dream of what you really are. A thought that you are apart from your Creator. A thought system based on specialness to protect itself. A wrong minded attempt to perceive yourself as you wish to be rather than as you are."]

In this model your intuition, the Source that surrounds and permeates you, is free to flow, to see things differently, to realize the love that is always there within you.

My story is of surviving uncommon childhood trauma and drama, some of which I invited. I was able to use it as a solid foundation to overcome every delusion that my small mind could conjure.

Through excruciating circumstances, including mental, physical, spiritual, and emotional pain, I finally chose again, determined to come out the other side. I chose to evolve. It took three decades. It is my hope that my story and the steps in this book can bring you to a place of healing and authenticity more quickly than it has taken me. Or perhaps it shall serve to usher you more directly on a journey you've already begun.

# Part I: Earth School

# Chapter I: Living Hell

"...the Holy Spirit... sees the world as a teaching device for bringing you home."

- *A Course in Miracles*

Struggle seems to appear in all our lives. Some of us are given hard lessons in youth which, if they don't serve to destroy us, may actually act as catalysts ushering us back home. For me those lessons were provided in the form of surviving a series of unstable childhood experiences. My father, a multi-talented genius tormented by mental illness, would without warning mercilessly and brutally beat my siblings and me regularly. You could almost set your watch to it. Out of the blue we would be picking ourselves up off the floor from a smack that had landed us up against the wall. However, he usually used the belt that he kept within reach on the arm of his favorite chair. He seemed to need to blow off this steam of built up pressure every few days or so, and his children were his outlet. When an outburst didn't happen for longer than that, we lived in fear, walking on eggshells, waiting for his next insane episode.

Mom and dad both chain-smoked, and both suffered from debilitating depression. I am quite sure now that they were also dependent on, if not addicted to, pharmaceutical medications. Dozens of pill bottles lined their medicine chest.

For as long as I can remember, my beloved mother, bless her soul, was gripped by paralyzing sorrow. The stress of our circumstances took its toll on her health as well. By the age of 29, a failed surgery to improve her hearing left her almost deaf. On top of that she had "off the charts" high blood pressure. She could not think of leaving my father. As so many women in abusive situations have found while also rearing young children, my mother had no means to support us. She was trapped. Trapped economically and trapped in her own beliefs that her life must be normal. I learned to keep my distance from mom for her emptiness seemed to consume me, which, of course, I hadn't the skills to escape.

As a very sensitive and shy child I frequently broke into tears at the drop of a hat. To complicate matters, crying even after punishment was unacceptable. Failure to hold back tears was accompanied by the threat of being beaten harder. The first spanking of my life was not for crying but rather for dropping food from my highchair like most babies do to learn about their world, i.e. gravity. I was eight months old. I'm told I was also awakened every two hours and force fed by my father as an infant. This was probably prompted by the backward ways of the medical profession in those days and his irrational fear that he had no choice lest I perish of starvation.

My father later drilled into my head as the eldest that I was responsible for the safety of my siblings. I adopted this role very seriously and accepted the responsibility of protecting my siblings at a very young age. I felt this my duty due to my mother's weakened physical condition and despondent state. This colossal burden included trying to keep them from being harmed by him too. I became hypervigilant to make sure no one upset daddy, which was impossible because we never knew when he'd fly off the handle.

In the seventh grade my gym teacher got a glimpse of the black and blue raised welts across my legs, bottom and back. Although she gave me a look of horror and pity, to my knowledge she never reported it. These are just a few accounts of the prolonged mental, emotional and physical trauma that my siblings and I endured. Mom wasn't excluded. She, too, was at the receiving end of dad's violent episodes. However, in all honesty, the physical attacks were not as scarring as the all too frequent mental and emotional torment that we endured.

My father was a mentally tortured soul, and he projected onto us, instilling into our heads how intrinsically bad, worthless and inadequate we were. He suspected that we were up to no good at every turn. As strange as it sounds, we had to enter my father's world of mental illness just to survive. I would at times tell a lie and sacrifice myself for him to feel in the right. Yet I adored my father. He was sick, and I felt a bizarre compassion for him. Somehow, even as a small child, I recognized the crazed fear in his eyes and the pain that drove his actions. I deducted that maybe I could help to heal my father if I just tried hard enough. If I was really good in school, or pretty enough, or talented enough, then maybe daddy would get better and everything would be okay.

I came home from kindergarten one day with a school math problem. He decided to help me with it. As a five-year old, the words he used to explain how to solve the problem seemed foreign to me. I didn't understand, nor could I, with all that pressure being put upon me. He hollered at me again and again, "Do you understand?" He slapped me across the face repeatedly as I said, "No," for I didn't know what the word "understand" meant and thought that was what he wanted to hear. He yelled louder and slapped me harder. Finally, I had the wit to say, "Yes, I understand," realizing the correct answer was yes. "Yes," even though I did not understand, and with that the beating stopped. I did not understand in reality, especially my father's erratic behavior.

We lived in poverty, and despite my father's ability to learn and master skills almost instantly, he didn't keep a job long. I am quite certain this led to his need for a geographical change every year or two. He was in three mental institutions for several months at a time during my childhood. My mother couldn't work with four children under the age of nine and one on the way. She was anxious all the time over getting the bills paid and was constantly asking dad for money for his debts in addition to necessary living expenses. She didn't obtain her driver's license until years later and found herself totally dependent on him. Accepting help from others in the community was not an option, and due to frequent moves and embarrassment over our circumstances, she managed to keep herself isolated.

I have a painful memory of some men coming to our home while my father was hospitalized for mental illness. They were repossessing our belongings due to unpaid debts that my father had accumulated. They even took our small tabletop organ. It was a gift from our grandparents and one of our most prized possessions. When my father was employed, he would often squander money on his hobbies. A sportsman by nature, he collected guns, was an accomplished archer, and loved deep sea and fly fishing. On the upside, wild game and fish meant food on the table. However, these hobbies demanded expensive paraphernalia. At one point, he even bought a horse, joined a horse-club and became its president.

Despite the extreme dysfunction at home my father was revered by his friends. His secrets of mental illness and domestic violence were safe. Or were they his secrets? I remember once choking down tears on the couch after a violent episode. My father in his recliner moments later looked over at me quizzically and asked, "What's wrong honey?" as if he hadn't just beaten us, in a fit of rage, moments before. Was he having total lapses of memory during these violent episodes? Was he a victim too?

# Chapter 2: Uprooted Again

"Nothing can destroy your peace of mind because God goes with you wherever you go."

– *A Course in Miracles*

Our family's last move was a big one. We trekked from Northern California to Colorado in 1973 during the tail end of the Vail Ski Area building boom. I would be entering my freshman year of high school in a new state. My father was able to obtain work as a finish carpenter, and with that better income, my parents purchased a bigger house trailer. We thought we were finally on easy street.

On the three-day drive to Colorado, I lectured my brother Billy, stressing to him the need to begin turning over a new leaf now that we were making a fresh start in Colorado. Billy was a year younger than me, and like many siblings, we had a love-hate relationship. We fought often yet we loved to hike and explore together. I was a bit of a tomboy and learned a lot by watching him. He taught me how to throw a perfect football spiral and how to place a baseball by changing my stance. We had a unique bond with a wonderful mutual respect that only siblings can truly know. Billy was red-headed like my mother, and he was all boy, athletic and perhaps a bit hyper. He met with more of our father's wrath than the rest of us due to his energetic nature. My father would say "sit still," and Billy simply could not.

Almost a year had passed since our arrival in Colorado, and Billy was nearing the end of his eighth-grade year. On May 22nd in 1974, I was doing my algebra homework in the living room when Billy arrived home from school. He seemed despondent, flinging his head against the back of the chair that he sat in adjacent to mine. We sat in silence for a short while when I became aware that something was not right and flippantly asked, "What the hell is wrong with you?" He didn't answer and, without me noticing, disappeared into my parent's bedroom.

A few moments later, I heard an earth-shattering explosion. The assault to my ears dumbfounded me. Reeling, my mind instantly flashed back to a couple of years before when Billy had lit the stove pilot light with a resulting small explosion. Luckily though, he had only been thrown across the room, and no one was hurt on that occasion. Terror brought me back into the moment, and I staggered to the source of the explosion. I found my brother on the floor, dead from a gunshot to the head. He'd known plenty about guns and in his despair had located, loaded, and literally blew his brains out with my father's Three-Fifty-Seven pistol.

How could this happen? Wasn't I in charge of keeping him safe? What a deafening blow to all of us. We were a family now stricken with the horror of suicide. No one took it harder than my mother who seemed almost catatonic with grief for months. In retrospect, I am uncertain if she ever recovered from losing her charming Billy.

Soon after, our father entered counseling. He was making an earnest effort to change. Through professional counseling I watched him miraculously transform his life for the better. He even put forth the effort to involve himself in our lives. I will always treasure that period because he taught me how to play tennis. I remember him being uncharacteristically patient when I would repeatedly miss the ball. When I did hit the ball, it would lob over the fence time and time again. This was a father I'd never known. I was finally getting the positive attention and quality time that every child craves. Although his transformation was short lived, it proved to me that people can change, even my dad.

Billy escaped the abuse in his own way. Now it was our turn. My sisters, Jackie (two years younger) and Pam (three years younger), made numerous attempts to flee the situation by running away from home. Jackie, not even fourteen yet, hitchhiked a thousand miles all the way back to Northern California. She showed up at my Aunt's doorstep and never returned. Pam, who set out to go with her, ended up back home to face dad's fury alone.

What was my escape plan? I decided, like my best friend Karen, to get pregnant, then I would have to get married, right? It had worked for her, as she appeared happy living independently of her parents. At the time it seemed like a good idea. I was going mad living under the war-like conditions at home and I wanted to survive. When it dawned on me what a mistake it was to get pregnant, it was too late. I got married at the tender age of sixteen, marrying the brother of my best friend's young husband. Five months later, now seventeen, I became a mother.

As a young mother, I was determined to raise my son right. I vowed that I would never make the mistakes my parents did. Parenting a child seemed like a monumental responsibility. Even so, I felt I was up to the task. I had a mission to make right my parents mistakes. I studied child rearing techniques and read book after book on the subject. However, as my newborn son Jeremy grew into toddlerhood, I found myself snapping into an insane state and striking out violently just like my father had. This completely horrified and confused me. How could I do what I swore I would never do? How could I repeat what my father did to me? What was wrong with me? Was my father's affliction hereditary?

I trusted my therapist with this secret. Little did I know admitting my lack of control meant that I would be visited by social services. I got a stern wakeup call when I got a knock on the door a few days later. This home visit with the kindhearted woman from social services so shamed and humiliated me that the violent behavior toward my precious son was all but snuffed out. Thank goodness.

Meanwhile, my new husband was rarely home. He was consumed with working and drinking too much. Unlike my best friend Karen, I hadn't escaped into a better life but merely went from the frying pan into the fire, as they say. The marriage began to deteriorate. There was another unplanned pregnancy which ended in miscarriage. My thinking at the time was misguided as I contemplated that if we were to have another baby, this time planning it, perhaps this might save the marriage. Our third pregnancy resulted in our beautiful baby girl, Jacinda. Her big brother was almost three when she was born. Now we had the perfect family, or at least it seemed that way for a brief while.

However as angelic as she was, my hope filled plan didn't work. It did not salvage our marriage and probably only postponed the inevitable. Over the next eight years the marriage worsened. I sunk deeper into depression and binge eating while he sunk deeper into alcoholism and marijuana use. As I got sicker, bulimia, exercise addiction, and even a bout of anorexia ensued.

# Chapter 3: My X and My Y

"Your passage through space and time is not at random. You cannot but be in the right place at the right time."

- *A Course in Miracles*

Spackled amongst the hard times were joyous moments, cherished memories, and both fearsome and futile attempts at marriage counseling. However, the writing on the wall led us to finally dissolve our marriage after a messy eleven years. We were both traumatized children ourselves, masquerading as adults, while all along attempting to raise two innocent, beautiful children. My hope is that Jeremy and Jacinda will remember the good times fondly.

In my anguish and desperate need of healing, I sought spiritual help. I had an inborn spiritual curiosity, and it was coming into full bloom. I continued attending the local church and reading the Bible. My therapist practiced Buddhism and taught me how to meditate, to which I took to like a fish in water.

In the throes of the divorce I had also developed a drinking habit on top of my bulimia. I left an alcoholic and took up drinking?! Due to rushing into the responsibilities of motherhood in high school, I had skipped the usual alcohol experimentation. I soon joined the local softball league, partly because I wanted to recapture the innocence, fun, and freedom of youth that had been stifled. Softball was synonymous with "partying" in our town, and I was subsequently introduced to the bar scene which included drugs.

A flummoxing dichotomy was realized. Addiction stems from spiritual disconnection or void, and I was well on my way. Like a lost wanderer in a burning desert, I was desperately searching for an oasis that would bring me some semblance of happiness and peace. My existence pendulated from binging/purging with food, alcohol/drugs and promiscuity, to eating tofu and salads, attending church, studying spiritual philosophy, and practicing daily meditation.

It was during this period in my life, in 1989, that a bar acquaintance and softball teammate asked me politely, then nearly begged me, to join the *A Course in Miracles* year-long study group that was starting in town. I wouldn't have done it without her unwavering persistence. Little did I know she was introducing me to the spiritual philosophy that would become the foundation of my life.

Somehow, I managed to obtain and hold a good job in the dental field while doing the best that I could, under the circumstances, to raise my children. However, I was overworked as a dental assistant, managing food and alcohol hangovers, and now remarried to another big drinker and former drug dealer. Somewhat embarrassed, I would jokingly quip to friends that my first marriage was my X and my second was my Y. Why did I marry him? In all honesty, between playing softball and partying, we had fallen deeply in love.

In the middle of this demise, one late night, I had a spiritual awakening. A vision came to me. I was in the center cog of spokes on a wheel. Other people were at the ends of each spoke, including God. I saw myself as the center of the universe. In a flash of lightning the vision dramatically mutated. Now Jesus resided in the middle and I joined the other people at the end of the spokes. Like an earthquake this shook and shifted the foundation of my entire world. I walked into my first Alcoholics Anonymous meeting a week later.

# Chapter 4: Outgrowing Trauma

"Those who remember always that they know nothing, and who have become willing to learn everything, will learn it."

- *A Course in Miracles*

The Alcoholics Anonymous meeting was held in the basement of the Methodist Church that I had formerly attended. Walking down those basement steps and through that door took enormous courage. I thought I would faint before I found my seat. There were five bikers all dressed in leather, most smoking cigarettes and drinking coffee. One was a hard-looking woman, and despite her tough exterior, I recognized a genuine softness in her eyes. Once seated, in spite of the appearance of the group, I never felt more welcomed, accepted, and loved. I sensed a profound serenity that filled the room like a timeless glow, and I knew in that moment that I truly wanted what they had.

When it was my turn to share, I didn't state that I was alcoholic but instead quoted something from the *Alcoholics Anonymous Big Book*, thinking I had outwitted the shame of admitting that I needed help. Suddenly, the biggest and most intimidating man of the bunch burst into laughter in response to my carefully chosen words. His laughter went on for a long while. I was shocked and humiliated by his seeming insensitivity. That was my entry into Alcoholics Anonymous, and though it was an awkward first step, my journey of ***outgrowing trauma*** began in that church basement. I had my last drink on New Year's Eve of 1992.

Doing the recommended step work of Alcoholics Anonymous was tortuous as I had to squarely look at my wrongs. My many mistakes glared at me while maintaining a fragile sobriety. In the past, drinking would douse the pain when feelings of guilt would surface, but this was no longer an option. Thankfully, I had a sponsor who had been down that road before, and she gently walked me through this agonizing time of rigorous self-reflection.

I had been exposed to the twelve steps through Al Anon, Overeaters Anonymous, and now Alcoholics Anonymous. I was sober, and by divine influence my life had been rerouted from its destructive course. I hadn't had a drink or drug in 55 days when I met with one of the deepest, darkest depressions I had ever known. I recall it was just a day or two before my 33rd birthday in late February. In the midst of this debilitating spiritual crisis I pined, "Who do I follow? Buddha, Jesus, another guru or something else entirely? How do I make this spiritual leap?" My habitual way "out" was taken away from me, and to make matters worse, since sobriety I hadn't experienced one good night's sleep. Insomnia plagued me for an entire year. It was tortuous. Perhaps the alcohol had acted as a sleep aid too.

On that frigid winter day, in this very, very dark state of mind, I was alone working late at the dental office. I was overwhelmed with tasks at work resulting from an extraordinarily busy day. I was sterilizing a mountain of dental instruments when a quote from a book by Brother Lawrence came to mind, "Do everything you do for the Love of God." All I could do in my despair was repeat this line from the book over and over and over again. "I'm doing this for the love of God, I'm doing this for the love of God ...the love of God." Every dental instrument I picked up and cleaned I would say these words again and again... repeating again and again. I was in a trance.

Suddenly, out of the corner of my eye in the adjacent operatory I experienced an apparition. Jesus Christ was there putting the sterilized dental instruments away. He appeared before me as real as if you were standing before me right now. He was shorter and stockier than I had imagined, dressed in a robe and sandals. At the sight of this vision, like a gushing waterfall, tears streamed profusely down my face. This was a miracle, you see, for I hated God for everything. I hadn't cried since I was a child as tears had just dried up at some point long ago. I was incapable of shedding a single tear, yet there I was crying! I was crying.

Unmistakably, my sought-after spiritual question had been answered. I knew exactly who to follow, and suddenly *A Course in Miracles*, a book of channeled messages from Jesus

Christ, came to the forefront of my mind. This was without a doubt the right path for me. Not religion or church but a spiritual philosophy. I saw a clear vision of Jesus at every Alcoholics Anonymous meeting that I attended sitting cross legged on the floor, following that apparition in the office. Tears would trickle down my face each time. Tears of hope, tears of love, and tears of the promise of recovering myself.

## Chapter 5: Another Blow

"It's not up to you to change your brother, but merely to accept him as he is... Any attempt you make to correct a brother means that you believe correction by you is possible, and this can only be the arrogance of the ego."

- *A Course in Miracles*

Another very late phone call from my sister, Jackie. She had a habit of calling while intoxicated, and her words would be filled with anger or remorse. I listened intently each time, feeling it was my obligation. Maybe, somehow, I could help. Afterall, I got sober so perhaps she could too. The phone calls were a common occurrence. Every time we hung up, I would feel so small and inadequate. I was her big sister and even though she was a thousand miles away, shouldn't I have had what it takes to help?

After one of these calls I casually mentioned to our youngest sister, Pam, that we would probably find Jackie dead in a ditch someday. Though a part of me felt that I had abandoned her, I decided not to answer her calls any longer as Al Anon prescribed. I received another phone call from Pam not long after I made my resolve not to take Jackie's calls. It was a month almost to the day since the apparition of Jesus in the office. Pam poured out how Jackie had been found dead along the side of a road a few days before. She'd had no identification, so police hadn't known until days later who she was or whom to notify.

Jackie had last been seen alive leaving a bar with a man she had dated in the past. With no witnesses, the supposition was that after a violent altercation with this man, she was either pushed or jumped out of his speeding vehicle. The impact had killed her instantly. My little sister, mother of three, was gone.

Oddly, I recalled that on March 24, 1992, I had beaten a punching bag with a plastic baseball bat in a fit of anger until I completely exhausted myself not knowing why. This incident correlated with the actual morning of Jackie's death. Was there a knowing somehow? I fully believe even now that Jesus appeared to me to give me the strength to bear this loss sober. I needed God now more than ever for I had lost my own mother when I was only 20. Five years after Billy's suicide, she had died of a heart attack while in the midst of a divorce that dad initiated, less than three weeks after Jacinda, her first granddaughter, was born. Mom would have been 39 that summer. I shall never forget the phone call I made to Jackie still in California, separated from her mother and only two weeks away from celebrating her 18th birthday. I was elected the bearer of the devastating news that her mother was gone. I was not prepared for her total and complete breakdown as she collapsed wailing uncontrollably into the phone. I felt utterly helpless and can only hope that Aunt Della was there to catch and console her.

Eight years later dad was diagnosed with cancer at the age of 47. Doctors gave him only two months to live, and he passed away four months later. I was at work when Pam called with the news that he had passed away in the night. Reverberations run through my body still when I hear the song that was playing in the background on the radio at that precise moment:

> "While there is time
> Let's go out and feel everything . . .
>
> For time is a river rolling into nowhere
> We must live while we can
> And we'll drink our cup of laughter
>
> The finer things keep shining through ..."

I am convinced this was a message for me from beyond. Every time I hear the song "The Finer Things" by Steve Winwood, I feel hope and joy and not loss. And sometimes I feel like dancing!

All of these deaths occurred in the span of seventeen years. Jackie was our fourth immediate family loss, and losing her too seemed impossible to accept. I struggled with pure disbelief. This cannot be happening! My old and twisted thinking simply could not or would not accept it. Didn't I have immunity from more loss after the preceding three deaths of those so close to me? Why?

Utterly dispirited, I felt as if I'd had the wind knocked out of my being. I was beyond help and drifted into a deep depression though I still had my sobriety by the grace of God. My sponsor and the fellowship of Alcoholics Anonymous literally carried me through this period. Whenever I was stricken with the urge to drink, I would call a sister A.A. member in need and offer to help her. I had to take the focus off of me because there was no earthly power that could save me, and I knew it. When I reached out to another in need, my cravings and problems would disappear. This is a key principle in the fellowship of A.A. related to sponsorship. When we commit to helping another through the steps of Alcoholics Anonymous, it keeps us sober too, and this is, in my view, precisely why A.A. works.

Weeks and months passed as I remained debilitated by grief. Every day in meditation I'd beg God for understanding. Why, why, why? Then one day while deep in meditation, I received an answer. A resounding voice that seemed to come from within said, "You do not have to understand." With these six ordinary words, I was released from the thousand-pound weight upon my heart. I experienced a peace around Jackie's death that truly surpassed all understanding. This mere shift in perception freed me.

# Chapter 6: A Spiritual Thread

"When a brother behaves insanely, you can heal him only by perceiving the sanity in him."

- *A Course in Miracles*

My journey to God was stifled. The epiphany I had around Jackie's death did not miraculously release me from other baggage. There was more work to do. The sunlight of the spirit was blocked by my inability to forgive my father. In my thwarted perception, he was the one who tortured us as children. He caused my brother's suicide. He made my mother's existence so stressful that she died. And yes, he was to blame for my little sister's plunge into alcoholism and certain death. In my mind he was a murderer. Death was not punishment enough.

Can you imagine my state of mind? I was seething with anger and resentment. And what about mom? Why didn't she stop him? Was she not an adult? In my pain and confusion, I lashed out wanting to blame someone, anyone. I knew all too well from being immersed in the principles of Alcoholics Anonymous that resentment leads to relapse. I could not afford to carry this grudge. I employed numerous rituals to shed my anger and resentment. Nothing worked. I knew I couldn't find any semblance of peace in the grips of hatred. I could not forgive, clinging to my rage like a frightened child, and it ate at me day and night.

Meanwhile, the high points that could peek out during this time were unforgettable. The kids and I were having the time of our lives. My second husband encouraged us to ski and snowboard and got us into various watersports including whitewater rafting. It was a whirlwind of excitement and bewilderment being married for the second time, though unfortunately it was doomed from the beginning. I had more than one friend try to talk me out of marrying again for obvious reasons which, apparently, I could not see. I struggled for another six years to remain sober while living with a practicing problem drinker.

My son could not live in the dysfunctional circumstances either. His stepfather was often irrational and domineering. Both with strong personalities, they locked horns on many occasions. Jeremy, an intelligent and gifted young man had himself emancipated through the courts when he was sixteen. He managed to graduate with his high school class. His own search via experimenting with drugs and alcohol eventually resulted in him enlisting in the Navy. In his need to distance from family and gain his independence, I would sometimes not hear from him for months at a time.

Just a couple of years later, in the same breath that my second marriage dissolved, my talented, and high achieving daughter, Jacinda, was awarded several scholarships to college. She chose the University of Northern Colorado on the front range to pursue her teaching degree just a few hours from home. During her second year of college, she became pregnant. However, she refused to let this derail her from her goal of obtaining her degree. I was so moved by her sheer determination that I committed a year to the cause, and without a second thought, packed up and moved to Northern Colorado. I dedicated the next twelve months to my daughter and her newborn baby.

This act was seen by family and friends as a heroic feat on my part. In all honesty, it also served as a desperate attempt for me to begin my life anew. I needed healing now more than ever, doing my best to recover from another failed marriage. I was still obsessed with finding the right man and, in my insane search for Mr. Right, exposed myself repeatedly to hurtful and often harmful situations. Furthermore, at nearly 40 years old, the unshakeable compulsion to binge eat was taking a toll on my health.

I was far from whole. My health was failing and depression was a constant. I knew from past experiences that I simply could not tolerate pharmaceutical medications. I needed an alternative if I was going to reclaim my health. In my search, I was led to a bioenergetic testing practitioner. Computerized bioenergetic testing measures electrical resistance through various acupuncture access points. This nonintrusive device is used to measure energy imbalances in the body that indicate what is lacking or needed to restore health. This discovery became the cornerstone for my overall improved health which quickly emerged into a passion to serve others, spurring a new career path that is still an integral part of my professional services today.

My first-born grandchild was brought into this world just before the summer solstice 1999. A beautiful, healthy baby girl. During this year of supporting my daughter and healing myself, I had an even greater resurgence to fully recover in body, mind, and spirit. Jacinda suggested I go back to *A Course in Miracles* meetings, but to my dismay, I couldn't find a meeting anywhere in the city.

I began to study on my own. It never failed every time I would open the book, though I rarely even understood what I was reading, I felt a strong calling and a strong remembering with each word on the page. My original *A Course In Miracles* teacher wisely advised her students to focus not on the words but the spaces between the words as we read. It was the space that bridged spiritual understanding. The words in this course were formatted to address the spirit within and not the analytical ego.

My desire to reside in the mountains grew stronger. As planned, I had stayed until Jacelyn's first birthday, and Jacinda was managing well as a new mom and thriving in school. I had fulfilled my year-long commitment to myself and to her. With her small family settled in place, I soon returned to reestablish a home back on the western slope of Colorado, just a few hours away from the girls, and secured a position in dentistry immediately.

A surprising result occurred: I was gifted with more joy, peace, and even better health when I was back in the mountains. Like a seedling bursting through the soil, I felt alive. I now believe that where we live is important as a human cannot flourish just anywhere. First on my agenda was to offer *A Course in Miracles* study. It was time to access and reconnect with my Source. This decision was for me as much as for the community. I soon began facilitating a small group in my home, committed to an even deeper spiritual journey.

# Chapter 7: For Giving

"The holiest of all the spots on earth is where an ancient hatred has become a present love."

- *A Course in Miracles*

While intensifying my study, I suddenly experienced the forgiveness for which I yearned.

Only love is real. When I gleaned from my studies of *A Course in Miracles* that only the love we gave or received is real, forgiveness happened of its own accord. No effort was required of me. In hindsight, the more I tried to forgive the more it eluded me, but when forgiveness happened of its own accord, a new and fresh perspective began flowing through me freely, renewing my soul.

Forgiving, according to *A Course in Miracles,* means to **give up** the erroneous beliefs of the egoic thought system. When I focused on, not the perceived horrors of my childhood but rather on the love that was given, the years of hate and resentment melted away. I instantly remembered mom waking almost every morning singing. She would wear a dress and heels regularly when I was little and always on holidays, even on Saint Patrick's Day. I remembered her love of babies and how she'd gather us round to tell us the heartwarming details of each of our births as we listened in awe. My parents would sing songs in the car on trips, and dad would take the time to teach us silly folk songs that he knew as a child. My sister Pam and I still remember some of these tunes. Dad would frequently test our math skills by launching into complicated verbal math problems: subtract this from that, add this, multiply that, divide this, and expect an answer. All in fun. I still smile when I reflect on the thrill of challenging our young minds. He would wrestle with us and throw us in the air and catch us. There was so much love given and so much received.

In a flash it occurred to me that this is all that is real. The rest is simply our earth school lessons. Lessons to come back to the love we never left. And like a shooting star my problem with non-forgiveness inexplicably vanished. I fully knew the truth, the love my parents extended. Yes, they experienced plenty of fear which colored my perception of their actions, but the love we shared will never die. When I knew this reality to my very bones, nothing else mattered. All the perceived trauma was just as illusory as a bad dream. Consequently, the grief of losing them lessened too. This was an enormous barrier removed. Yes, I was free, but please keep in mind, this new attitude is far from a disregard for my own self-protection in potentially harmful situations. It's more along the lines of making a different choice, and so now, when faced with a hypothetical oncoming truck, I choose instead to extend love as I gently step out of the way.

This prayer, taken from bits and pieces of my studies helps me when I fall back into anger, sadness, confusion, or fear regarding a family member, another person, institution, or authority:

> I love you (person, institution) ____________________
> as I remember God's love.
>
> I am upset because I see something that isn't there.
>
> Please help me, Holy Spirit, to see beyond this lie, this misperception, to the beauty, love and light that is here in truth.
>
> Thank you for my holiness, for your (person, institution, etc.) ______________________ holiness and for God's perfect forgiveness.
>
> AMEN

# Chapter 8: Beyond the Veil

"The journey to God is merely the reawakening of the knowledge of where you are always, and what you are forever."

- *A Course in Miracles*

Do you have visions, prophetic dreams or premonitions? I didn't know everyone didn't have extrasensory encounters. I'd been having them since I was a little girl. It came to my attention during *A Course in Miracles* meeting when I shared my experiences and the group was astounded. The vision at the dental office in 1992 that fortified my recovery and directed my spiritual path was the most moving.

Another vision: A picture of Jesus on the wall came alive. When I was practicing yoga one morning the picture became three-dimensional and appeared right in front of my face. It was so close to my face it was as if I was becoming one with Christ. Naturally, this frightened me, and yet in that split second I had the presence of mind to ask for the fear to be removed. The awesome oneness lingered a while longer. I rode my bike to work that day and turned to view mountains in the distance. I blinked more than once because they were registering as one dimensional as if I was looking at a picture on the wall. This seemed quite strange until I arrived at the office to learn that a respected colleague, healer, and friend that shared space in the office had died unexpectedly in the night. My experiences that morning began to make sense in a nonsensical way.

A dream: Years before, I had a dream when my daughter was in high school. It was New Year's Eve and she was staying over with a friend. I went to bed that night and dreamed I was being told that Jacinda was at the bottom of a lake and that she would die. Deeply distressed, I asked God to take me instead and was given permission to proceed. I decided in that second to sacrifice my own life to save hers. I dove in what felt like icy water into a very eerily deep and dark bottomless crevice. There I found her and pushed her up further and further to the surface. Then I sunk into the depths to die. I awoke quite shaken by this dream.

Jacinda arrived home sometime in the afternoon. We were chatting and I said, "Honey, I had this really unsettling dream last night." As I poured out the story, she buried her face in her hands and sobbed. She said, "Mom you are so psychic," and went on to explain in detail how there had been an unsupervised party where she'd spent the night. There was a lot of drinking. She had passed out in the hot tub and no one had noticed. Miraculously, one of her inebriated classmates saw her submerged and pulled her out of the hot tub just in time to save her life.

A dream: I was in a foreign country on the side of a steep mountain. It was an emerald green landscape, crisp and cold. There was a three-story house built on the side of a mountain, and it was burning to the ground. I was frantically carrying blonde children out of the house to safety, one after the other. One, two, three and more. I worked madly to get them out of the house. I woke up physically exhausted as if I had really been there. I had planned to jog that morning with a girlfriend, and she flipped on the radio right after I'd told her about my dream. We both listened with utter astonishment as the headliner news announced that an entire family of nine in Switzerland perished in a fire in their home as they slept. Was I there, somehow, perhaps helping them to crossover?

A dream: Another dream years later shook me to my core. I was laboring again very hard, this time in some sort of bunker. There was a horrific battle being fought. I was on the ground tending to wounded, who were not native Americans but a more ancient people, one after the other. My job in the dream was obvious. I was assisting them in transitioning to the next life. I held them in my hands and stayed with them while their spirit moved out of their bodies. I felt my hands soaked with warm, sticky blood. It felt so real, as if I went back in time to play some crucial part in an ancient bloody battle.

Immediately after Jacelyn's birth, my incredibly strong daughter Jacinda began hemorrhaging, losing a tremendous amount of blood. She eventually called out and fainted. I whisked her newborn to the nurse so that I could aid Jacinda. In that instant, out of the corner of my eye a blur of four or six cherub-like angels zipped into the room from the left corner of the ceiling and planted themselves around her bed. She recovered in record time without receiving the recommended blood transfusion.

A vision: When my son was in the Navy in Pensacola, sometimes I would not hear from him for months or even a year at a time. In my mind's eye, I would see him alone and scared on a dark path. A foot or so above him I would see the vision of a tiny golden-haired angel with a bow and arrow cocked, like a luminous sentinel vigilantly protecting him from harm. I still see her when I feel concern for him long distance. I never told Jeremy about this vision. I wonder if he senses her too.

Visions: When I'm working with clients I see energy or light move around and through them. I often see what might be guardians or angels in the upper corner of the room. I hear a voice directing me to just listen or to do a specific exercise with them as I am serving them. Again, I don't pretend to understand these experiences. I note them.

Some may call these mystical encounters special gifts, but in my experience all of us have unique connections to the divine. Who hasn't had a hunch that was right on, thought of an old acquaintance and gotten a phone call from that very person, or was simply, inexplicably, in the right place at the right time to change the course of their life for the better? Mysticism, in and of itself, is not the end all, but it can be either appreciated when it arrives or sought after. In my humble opinion, the latter becomes just another egoic wild goose chase distracting you from the love and light that is shining in you now.

Sharper intuition is magnified by removing the clutter from our hearts and minds and our experiences. It is about being willing and open to learn how to let go of what is no longer working and to trust a higher presence. This requires learning from your circumstances and everything that has happened in your life. I invite you to journey with me in the coming pages. There you may recognize yourself and realize that you too can make lasting life changes.

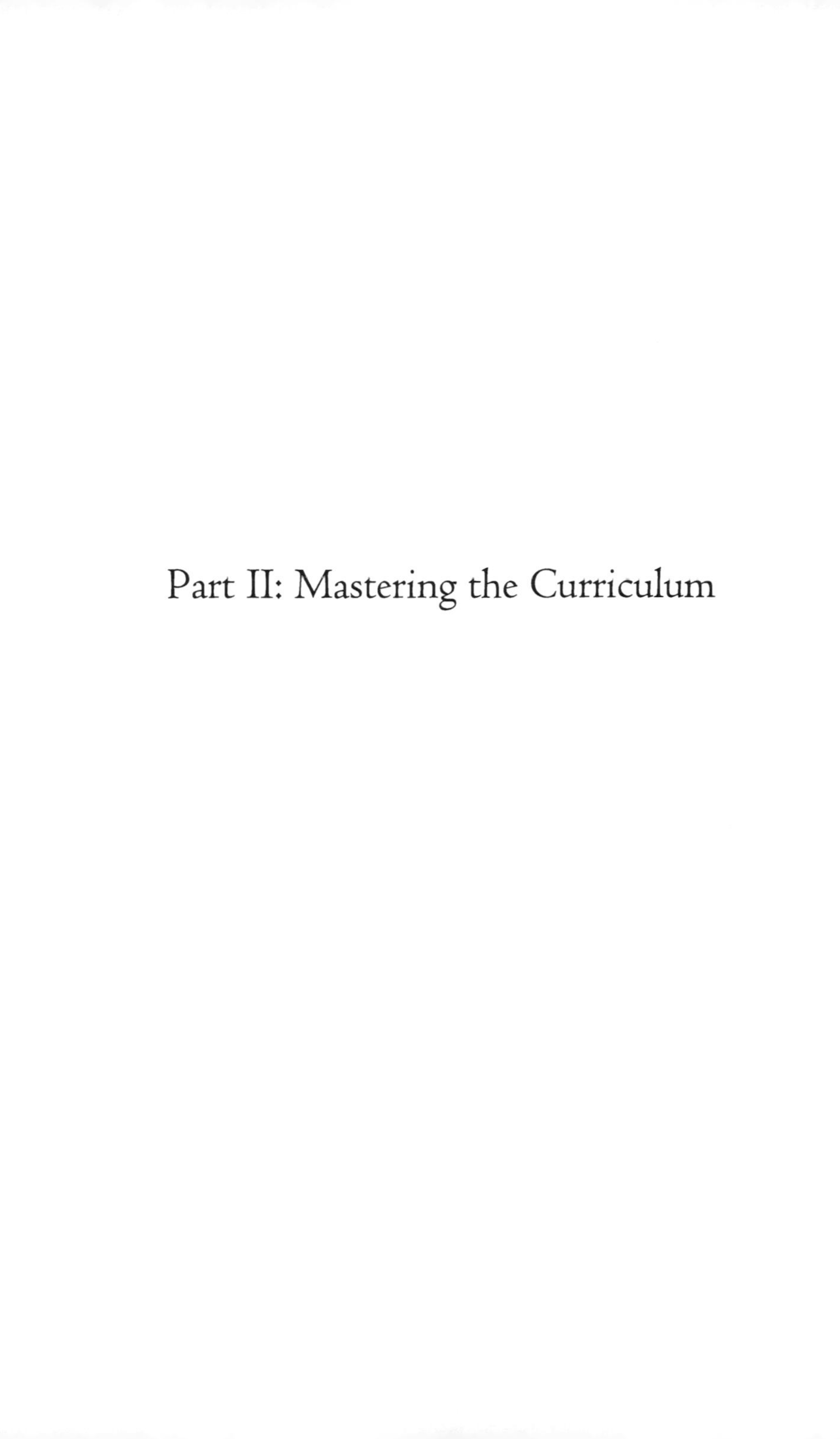

# Part II: Mastering the Curriculum

# Chapter 9: I'm Not Enough

"... the Course deals with universal spiritual themes. It emphasizes it is but one version of the universal curriculum. There are many others, this one differing from them only in form. They all lead to God in the end."

- *A Course in Miracles*

Our little group grew. More were attending the *A Course in Miracles* meetings. We expanded from meeting in my humble abode to the office where I was now a practicing certified bioenergetic technician. I had a simple format for the meetings and followed it, though I felt quite inadequate as a facilitator. I really knew nothing, having no credentials except my own study and practice. This seemed a heavy and serious responsibility to the group and to God.

I was wrestling with the higher concepts laid out in the course so continued to lean on my first teacher's approach. Although I didn't grasp the *A Course in Miracles* concepts fully, I steadfastly followed her format from years before and kept showing up. Truth be told, I felt like a fake. I was in a place of extreme recrimination for I could not seem to practice these principles consistently at home, nor could I remember them at times. How could I possibly lead others? In hindsight, what was blocking me was my own egoic irrational thoughts. Thoughts such as, "Who am I to lead others?"

Clumsily, I pressed on with my struggle to connect with my own inner Guide. My facilitating became passive. I would follow the format rigidly, listen compassionately, and intuitively invite the next person to share. Plagued with self-doubt and inadequacy, I would leave the meeting emotionally stressed. It would manifest in my chest as I would struggle to breathe on my way home from nearly every meeting. It was similar to an asthma attack and would last an hour or so. Ironically, I would receive compliments for skillfully and intuitively facilitating the group.

Because my own life was far from peaceful, every couple of years or so I would take a sabbatical for a few months and often up to a year at a time. The group would disperse, confused and feeling a bit abandoned and sometimes angry. Little did they know, I feared falling off of the pedestal where I felt I had been placed, and taking a break was for my own self-preservation.

It was during these breaks from our group that I began reading other spiritually-based self-help books. I developed the ability of recognizing truth and sifting through those ideas that did not align. The books and audios that resonated, I studied and took copious notes. Unbeknownst to me, my studies were the beginnings of formulating a series of articles, workshops, and programs to help others like myself reconnect with their own inner Guide.

A Course in Miracles states that there are many roads to God. Through applying my studies, perhaps I could provide practical application for seekers who were turned off by the depth or use of Biblical terminology utilized in *A Course in Miracles.* It is important to point out that for those seriously considering ACIM, it is not a religious text but rather a non-dualistic spiritual philosophy based on love.

Some of the texts and audios I explored which supported these concepts were *The Presence Process, The Big Book of AA, The Power of Now,* Rumi, *The Sedona Method, My Stroke of Insight, Loving What Is,* and many, many more. Please see my bibliography for a more thorough list. These philosophies had one thing in common: they were all ego deflating and spiritually grounding and thus sound under my sagacious examination.

It is also paramount to share that at this point in my life, I had finally happily remarried as I was ready for a stable and loving partnership. We had been acquaintances for several years in the A.A. program. Along with being kind and possessing a generous heart, like me, he was living in recovery. This was a welcomed change. Dwayne, my husband, has been my best teacher and soul mate in this time of spiritual growth. Our journey has been full of ups and downs, and we have both endured and grown beyond our expectations. I could write another book on the many loving gifts Dwayne has given me. He accepts me just as I am. He always has. He accepts my family and family dynamics – the good, the bad, and the ugly. In the drama of family events, he has a knack for putting it all into perspective. He is gifted with the ability to bridge harmony in the midst of opposing views. He is always there to help. He is there for my kids, my grandkids, and even Jackie's kids, my niece and nephews. If someone is in need, he is there. Dwayne is my best friend.

# Chapter 10: An Ocean of Emotion

"For to recognize fear is not enough to escape from it, although, the recognition is necessary to demonstrate the need for escape... Yes, we have repeatedly emphasized the need to recognize fear and face it without disguise – is a crucial step in the undoing of the ego."

– *A Course in Miracles*

As I began my journey of healing, my empathic tendencies became heightened. I remember walking into a room and feeling everything. When I was near my husband, especially as we went to bed at the end of the day, vibrations of emotion such as anger would take hold of me and keep me from sleeping. I was convinced that I was a victim of his suppressed emotions.

I did various emotional release techniques. I practiced and became proficient in "tapping" for a year or two. Tapping is an alternative treatment for physical pain and emotional distress. It is also referred to as psychological acupressure. People who use this technique believe that tapping the body can create a balance in one's energy system and alleviate pain.

Although tapping worked, something about it did not fully resonate with me. It identified the feeling, but I didn't have to consciously work with the emotion other than to just tap it away. I felt there was a missed opportunity to heal at a deeper level.

The Sedona Method required that I feel and allow the emotion and get the full force of the healing by breathing into it. By diving into the energy of the emotion, I was permanently healing a lifetime of emotional baggage – one feeling at a time. This necessitated that I tune in more to myself, and it just felt right. It wasn't until I began practicing the emotional release that I was studying that I came to realize the feelings I was picking up from others were simply a projection of my own unprocessed fears and heavy bag of repressed emotion.

It was so much easier to blame those closest to me for the tumultuous ups and downs I was experiencing. This pattern can keep us stuck and distract us from our growth. We are afraid to own our emotions lest they consume us, and so our knee-jerk response is to project it onto those closest to us. Fear of surfacing emotion is an enormous barrier to accessing the peace within. I can attest to this wholeheartedly.

The old way of coping with surfacing emotion was to shield myself against all the energy floating around me in the ethers. Protect myself with this trinket or that elixir? Everybody was doing it, especially in the holistic healing field. But where is the growth in that? It left me feeling at the mercy of others and of situations over which I had no control.

I discovered at an even deeper emotional level in which what you resist persists. This statement is as sound as the physics of gravity. In other words, when we put up boundaries or a barrier, even energetically against something or someone, it only serves to make the charge stronger, bigger, and more glaring. When this concept really sunk in, like a lightbulb switching on in my head, I finally got it! From that point on when I felt anything, I took full responsibility for it. Afterall, I was the one feeling it. I had empowered myself to grow beyond and release all unprocessed emotion.

After that time of discovery, any emotion another was having that I picked up on became an opportunity for me to feel what it triggered emotionally in me and process it to my own better health. When I felt emotion welling up that I suspected was originating from my husband, or anyone else for that matter, I tuned into myself, identified my feeling, dove into it, and released it. Incidentally, my communication in all my relationships felt cleaner and less sticky as a result.

This was not an easy path for me. You see, I was terrified of my own buried emotion. My childhood experiences impacted how I dealt with emotion as there had been the threat of severe punishment in our household if we expressed emotion. As you may recall in my story, I learned at a very young age to swallow my tears. Being taught to suppress my feelings, I had no way of knowing how to process my feelings. As a sensitive child, I empathically absorbed the excessive buried emotions my parents were trying desperately to escape.

When I opened the gate to begin processing this old baggage, I was so emotionally overwhelmed that I couldn't even identify what I was feeling at a given moment. I was emotionally handicapped. I had to re-learn how to feel one emotion at a time. Once I became proficient in identifying my feelings, I incorporated these techniques into my practice. Through bioenergetic testing it was revealed what we have always known that – clients' health issues were worsened by suppressed emotion.

# Chapter 11: The Voice in My Head

"A holy relationship starts from a different premise. Each one has looked within and seen no lack. Accepting his completion, he would extend it by joining with another, whole as himself."

- *A Course in Miracles*

My clients were coming to me for bioenergetic testing with enthusiasm. However, when I introduced the emotional release practice, most were not interested. For years I would offer this piece with few takers. I continued to practice emotional release with myself and family.

Speaking of family, my children were young adults and both struggling in very different ways. Coincidentally, they both had bouts of depression. Moreover, I tended to take on a ludicrous belief that it was my fault and I should make their path easier. I felt guilty for every wrong thing that was going on in their world. I just felt compelled to fix it, and the best way I knew was to be there to listen and advise. I would drop everything to take their calls. This interfered greatly with living my own life and maintaining my marriage, friendships, and career.

Yes, I had been clean and sober for many years, yet I was plagued with fear and worry. I made myself sick with worry for my family members, my children, my own inadequacies, about money, and about my husband. Perhaps this was a combination of past trauma and egoic thinking. The list was endless.

I sacrificed for my adult children much like I had for my siblings, especially Jackie, when they had difficulties. I would torture myself with awful thoughts about what might happen to them almost every night as I lay in bed. This played havoc on my ability to sleep. In hindsight, I realize I was deep in the clutches of something called codependency (excessive emotional or psychological reliance on another; typically, one who requires support due to an illness or addiction).

Most of these thoughts were fear based. The voice in my head which I call the "small self" or the ego was keeping me in chains. I was living in "what if" on one hand and feelings of guilt on the other for what I did or didn't do while raising my children. If only I had been a better mother, then they'd be okay, right? I am sure this cyclical future and past thinking that had me by the throat aged me. It went on for years before I discovered another tool.

# Chapter 12: It's Just a Thought

"Guilt is a sure sign that your thinking is unnatural."

– *A Course in Miracles*

A friend of a friend from Al Anon mentioned how the four questions formula from *The Work* by Byron Katie was helping her to live with less guilt. I had heard about Byron many years before but had never taken the time to read her books. My small egoic-self wanted nothing to do with looking squarely at the stories going on in my head. Even though these were the very stories that kept me in chains, I was strangely attached to them. Not only that, but it sounded like a whole lot of work.

Why would I be attached to stories in my head? Well, I thought them and therefore they must be correct, right? Am I my thoughts? Nothing could be further from the truth, and confusion sets in when we mistake our thoughts with our identity. The ego or small self must be right at any cost, so it tricks us into thinking we are the myriad of ideas floating through our heads. When you question these thoughts, the ego deflates in that very instant and inspiration rushes in like a cool breeze on a summer day. Reframing cyclical thoughts is a crucial step in recovering your intuition and connection to Source.

Jill B. Taylor, in her *My Stroke of Insight: A Brain Scientist's Personal Journey*, shares: "I need to remember, however, that there are enormous gaps between what I know and what I think I know." She states repeatedly in so many words that the spirit knows while the ego only guesses. The idea that you can change your thoughts just seemed alien to me. I had heard Louise Hay say, "It's only a thought, and a thought can be changed," but how is that possible when studies reveal that we think as many as fifty to sixty thousand thoughts a day?

Despite my former opinion, I embraced the idea of examining my thoughts one at a time and changing it to a truer thought. This was a spiritual leap to examine a thought and challenge it against the facts. Just because I thought it doesn't make it true. It is my thoughts that stimulate erroneous assumptions, anger and worry, and impulsive actions, and they stress my physical health, which eventually all contribute to illness.

Once I got the hang of this work, I gleaned unbelievable results. I was able to challenge the ego thoughts that were keeping me stuck so I could then move on to kinder thoughts toward myself and others. Wow! When I began regularly dissecting my thoughts, my peace deepened incrementally. I studied and practiced diligently *The Work* for two years. At that point I contacted the author. She generously gave me permission to teach it and even surprised me with templates and resources to aid me sharing her brilliant formula with others.

Combined with the emotional release that I had gathered in my tool box, I created an affirmation that freed me from codependency, worry, and guilt, especially with regard to my adult children. It goes like this: "I allow my children to experience all that they do." With those words I am free. I fully embody the truth, for everything they experience is needed as part of their personal perfect journey back to God. No one can make this journey for us.

I wouldn't have gained the wisdom to live my purpose and passion today if I hadn't had my life experiences. Imagine how stunted and underdeveloped we would feel if someone had protected us from the challenging aspects of life. In my mind, it is a crime to interfere with the spiritual growth of another. To drive the point home, the immune system is weakened if overprotected. It is essentially boosted by being exposed to viruses, bacteria, dust, and the like. The very best act that I could do for Jeremy and Jacinda would be to allow them to experience, without interference, all that their life lessons would have to offer.

## Chapter 13: Resistance, A Dubious Luxury

"...Now is the closest approximation of eternity that this world offers. It is in the reality of 'now,' without past or future, that the beginning of the appreciation of eternity lies."

- *A Course in Miracles*

All of this was teaching me to embrace the now. If I was feeling emotion, I dove into experiencing it. If I was plagued with negative stories in my head, I'd dive into examining them. Yes, now is the portal to overcoming your personal barriers to peace.

My personal breakthroughs bled into working with clients. I was so excited about this new approach to our thoughts and emotions! Those who were not keen to diving into emotion, I would begin by guiding them through dissecting their thoughts. Some, like my husband, who shied away from emotional work, really preferred the process of examining their thoughts.

"Health is the result of relinquishing all attempts to use the body lovelessly."

- *A Course in Miracles*

Ill health is most definitely a barrier to connecting with Source. When we don't feel well, it can interfere with our growth. After a couple of years of clearing multiple layers of harmful agents exacted through bioenergetic testing using homeopathic and botanical remedies, I was free of debilitating allergy symptoms.

Have you ever or do you know someone who has experienced severe allergy symptoms? Allergy sufferers know how annoying and sometimes life threatening they can be. Symptoms can affect work, play, and everything in between. Some that I experienced were swollen itchy eyes, chronic congestion (my voice sounded nasal day and night), wheezing, coughing, and sneezing fits. When my natural histamines kicked in to counteract these symptoms, I would end up flat on my back with overwhelming fatigue. It was miserable and limiting. In a word, I was imprisoned.

Several years after my complete freedom from these symptoms due to the marvels of bioenergetic testing, I noticed a new physiological response. I began incorporating all of these new tools that I had garnered through my own trial and error. Additionally, when I slowed down and tuned into my body I discovered that certain foods contributed to my symptoms. As you read further, you will discover how mood, thought, and stress levels are all contributing factors. Finally, I had let this ailment go.

I was free to breathe and enjoy nature for several years. However, one spring night we had the bedroom windows open to let in the cool mountain breeze, and I felt the beginnings of allergy symptoms. My first reaction was to panic. "Oh no, I can't be going through this again!" went through my head. Instead of letting the panic go unchecked, I chose to dive into the sensations brought on by the onslaught of pollen in the air.

Once the symptoms started, there was nothing I could do to stop them. This I knew all too well. I was unwilling to go back to that hell, which meant to succumb to the tickling feeling in my nose and the itchy feeling in my eyes. I welcomed my honest resistance to these sensations as best I could, knowing my body knew what to do now that it was less burdened by layers of toxicity. I went deeper. I tried something radical: I sunk into the sensations even more, embracing every subtle nuance with full awareness.

I continued to allow the physical sensations, feelings of panic, and resistance until it began to melt away like snow on a spring day. I fully gave my conscious attention to it instead of losing myself. I had discovered, to my surprise, the act of welcoming the sensations and accompanying emotions can actually act as a segue back to calm in body as well as in spirit.

Within five minutes of trusting this process, every symptom disappeared. That never had happened before. The experiment was a success! I did not experience another full-blown allergic reaction the entire summer or since. In subsequent years, I have observed the fluffy cottonwood seeds pour down like snow around me and chosen not to get up in arms about it. I might sneeze once and then I move on. It's a normal response when pollen is floating in the air to sneeze once. From that day forward I have never been triggered again into that cycle of severe allergy symptoms. *

When you break it down, aside from a sneeze when dust is drifting around, isn't an allergic reaction the body's way of resisting to the extreme? I am certain that the decision to dive into my demise, rather than resist, is without question what got me out the other side. Were my mental thoughts that stimulated emotional resistance playing a part in exasperating or perhaps manifesting symptoms?

Asthma, on the other hand, was still a problem. It had probably lessened since that successful allergy experiment but still continued to limit my life. It reared its ugly head during physical exertion or exposure to cold weather, and it kept me from enjoying an active lifestyle. A colleague suggested that I come into the present moment during asthma attacks. This sounded counterintuitive as there is nothing more frightening than the feeling of suffocation. Was she crazy? She was asking me to welcome the wheezing as well as everything else that I was experiencing in that moment. Nevertheless, I did as she suggested, and the attack seemed to dissipate slightly. This required great focus, yet there was always a noticeable reduction in my symptoms. The more I practiced, the more relief I would get as my chest relaxed. I also noted that breathing through my nose really helped as well. Wow! Soon even asthmatic episodes became a limitation of the past.

Louise Hay states in her book, *You Can Heal Your Life*, that both allergies and asthma are related to emotional trauma. I found this interesting as the onset of both these maladies in my life had occurred in my preadolescent years.

* Please see your healthcare professional if you have trouble breathing or are experiencing other allergy symptoms.

# Chapter 14: The Gift of Pain

"It's not up to you what you learn, but only whether you learn through joy or through pain."

- *A Course in Miracles*

Ah yes, and then there was pain. The ultimate physical barrier. We've all known pain: a bladder infection, migraines, childbirth, kidney stones, surgery. I've had my share of physical pain, and because I was so highly sensitive to pharmaceutical medications I learned to live with pain. This interfered a great deal with my life, my relationships, my freedom, and my career.

As quoted previously, what we resist, persists. This famous quote by Carl Jung contends that "What you resist not only persists but will grow in size." Today this viewpoint is generally abbreviated to "What you resist persists." Jung was right. In my experience, every time I was able to consciously dive into the discomforting waves of pain, the throbbing, sharpness or dullness of it, it would lessen. I recall from years before how breathing into the discomfort was quite effective in childbirth and I believe shortened labor significantly. This practice took great discipline and tremendous focus. It seems, however, that the deeper I focused on it, the quicker this discipline would yield results. Of course I do not recommend this for acute issues, so please get necessary medical attention.

During the process of diving into these uneasy sensations and feelings, I would actually become curious about all I was experiencing, which was quite the opposite of resisting the pain. It worked every time to some degree, often completely dissipating. I would forget that I'd even had some pain a moment before. In this way pain is transformed and gives way to peace. Another wow! Even physical pain had an emotional tag.

"The only aspect of time that is eternal is now."

– *A Course in Miracles*

I was discovering the secret of the present moment. When I wasn't defending against anxiety, fighting pain, or trying to ward off allergies, I was diving in consciously and thus liberating myself. In other words, bringing the light of my conscious attention instead of resisting the uncomfortable. I was able to begin to free myself more rapidly.

I brought this practice to an old nervous habit. Excoriation disorder (also referred to as chronic skin-picking or dermatillomania) is a mental illness related to obsessive-compulsive disorder. It is characterized by repeated picking at one's own skin which results in skin lesions and causes significant disruption in one's life. I would pick at my skin until it sometimes bled. This strange disorder would remain dormant for years at a time. In my case it wasn't what I would call a severe issue, but I would catch myself picking at my skin during ordinary moments, especially while driving my car.

My husband, who loves me dearly, was horrified by this form of mutilation and asked me to find a way to stop. I tried everything but could not. Obviously, I was powerless over this. I took the next step and examined it closely and saw a pattern when I took a good look at it. I realized it was always stimulated by my thoughts. Again, our thinking can distract us from our connection to Source, especially egoic thoughts of the past and future. Often, in my case, it was in the immediate future like where I was headed to in the car.

I conducted another experiment: I focused on the present moment while driving. I noticed the feeling of the steering wheel, the textures of the interior of my car, the bug that splattered on the windshield, my body supported by the contours of the seat, the sound of the tires humming against the pavement, the road laid out before me, the warmth of the sun on the left side of my face, the scenery in the distance, the bird flying above. I thought I had coined this practice "ordinary moments". However, I discovered later that the author of *The Way of the Peaceful Warrior* uses this very same term. Nevertheless, it is a sacred treat for my mind and spirit as opposed to the barrage of past and/or future mind chatter. Now, literally, I began accessing the realm of spirit, my higher Self, simply by utilizing my problems, whether it was thought, emotion or pain by coming into the now.

## Chapter 15: My Pot of Gold

"There is no darkness that the light of love will not dispel, unless it is concealed from love's beneficence. ... As darkness disappears in light, so ignorance fades away when knowledge dawns."

- *A Course in Miracles*

Ordinary moments were another cornerstone of connecting spiritually and became my pot of gold. In the present moment I found absolute peace. When I am fully experiencing the now, no matter what, I am pleasantly immersed into a serene state of mind. I have experienced peace even in the midst of perceived upset and chaos. While employing my new-found practice, the daily commute would seem to take less time. I would arrive refreshed and centered. All was well in this ordinary moment.

Consider this moment what you are experiencing: the words you are reading, the spaces between each word, the color of the page and the textures, the sound of your breath, the sounds in the distance, the contact points your body is engaging with on the chair, the feeling of your clothing touching your skin, even the empty space between your eyes and the page.

As a practitioner, I schedule ordinary moments into my day. It keeps me sane. Periodically, I set my cell phone alarm to go off midmorning and midafternoon during the day to gently remind me. I included "ordinary moments" while dining. This was key to reestablishing a healthy relationship with food. More on this in Part III.

Ordinary moments equate to embracing the present moment which is in essence a form of meditation. In my humble opinion, I think our small self or egoic self gets hooked on the overstimulating events and hates the illusory dullness of the current moment. Through a whole lot of distraction the ego is keeping a secret from us, and that secret is this: Ego is swallowed up by the present moment because the present is the realm of universal love, great spirit - God. Ego cannot survive in the light of the present moment.

Why not bypass ego distractions and bring the excitement of the now into what may have been perceived as a dull drive? A common denominator began to emerge. Not only was it in the now that emotion could be processed healthfully, it was only in the present moment that I could squarely examine a thought and see how preposterous it really was. The result was the presence of mind to reframe it in a way that felt truer and kinder. Kinder to who? Why to me, of course. I was the only one in my head being tortured by the lies my ego or small self was manufacturing. Only by slowing down and embracing what I was experiencing right now could healing occur.

"Those who seek the light are merely covering their eyes. The light is in them now. Enlightenment is but a recognition, not a change at all."

- *A Course in Miracles*

I had spent much of my young adult life in therapy, plagued with depression even as a child. I tried tapping, hypnosis and more. After years of practicing emotional release another piece of the puzzle fell into place. I was overcome with a dark, paralyzing depression. It seemed to come out of nowhere. I thought I was beyond this but here I was in the grips of a daunting depression once again. I had a dozen years of sound sobriety under my belt, better health, and now all these tools. Naturally, this frightened me because before I became sober, I had remained in the clutches of a seemingly inescapable depression for two years. I couldn't tolerate pharmaceuticals, and I also didn't want to end up like my parents, dependent on chemicals.

On this occasion, I did my best to utilize the tools that I had learned and tried very hard to let it go as best I could. However, I was so terrified by it that I was instead glazing over it and trying very hard to push it away. Resisting heavy emotion was an old pattern and I was doing it unknowingly once again. The last thing I wanted to do was welcome it. What if it took me over again? Somehow, I managed to keep it at bay, never fully embracing it. I was trying to release it without fully feeling it.

Somehow, in my angst I'd forgotten that we must feel it to heal it.

Sometimes there is a lesson in a surfacing emotion, a healing that you would miss if you just stuff it back into your heavy bag. If you are dedicated to self-evolution you don't want to miss the miracle of spiritual growth. Days went by and no matter what I told myself I could not shake this debilitating gloom and sorrow. I tried to maintain the status quo while navigating my world but this heavy emotion had me by the throat. I felt paralyzed.

Finally, one morning I marched into my room, fell to my knees, looked up, and said to God and the Universe, "If I have to feel this for the rest of my life, I will." I hung my head and surrendered fully for about two minutes in which that time seemed nonexistent. Suddenly the heavy depression completely and totally lifted. To my astonishment, it was gone just as mysteriously as it had arrived. Thus, fortifying the miracle of surrender.

# Chapter 16: The Final Pieces

"If you are trusting in your own strength, you have every reason to be apprehensive, anxious and fearful."

- *A Course in Miracles*

At this point you'd have thought that my process of healing was complete. But healing is more analogous to a journey. I discovered healing continually unfolds before us and is a process, not a destination. I knew something was missing. While I was continuing to utilize the marvels of bioenergetic testing to clear my clients and myself of toxins and assisting with meditation, emotional release, and reframing negative thoughts, it didn't yet feel complete. Something was missing.

As I pondered, the missing pieces trickled in with perfect timing through my own life lessons. Specifically, my two weak spots: my relationships with food and those who meant the most to me. The latter, as I knew from my studies, is the biggest opportunity for personal growth. And in that respect, I lovingly consider my easygoing husband, Dwayne, my biggest teacher.

Life was not balanced and was far from perfect, for my beloved and I were experiencing our share of marital strife. Yes, releasing pent up emotions and reframing negative thoughts helped us clear the air to some extent, but something more dynamic was needed. Like anything else destined to bloom, my desire to grow relationally led me to harnessing compassionate listening skills as well as acquiring the techniques and tools to discuss matters calmly. My mantra became "take nothing personally," and I credit that to helping my marriage thrive again. If I didn't have a sense of security at home, I wouldn't be able to give fully to others.

Navigating the physical world that we live in also included my relationship with food. Like a deeply entrenched groove that makes a vinyl record skip again and again, I had continued to use food to escape my worries and smother my fears. I did not have a handle on the old addiction to food. Yes, it was somewhat manageable, but it was still rearing its ugly head. In some ways recovering from alcohol addiction was easier as I could divorce alcohol by abstaining altogether. However, I had to eat to fuel my body, and this meant I needed to rebuild and maintain a healthy relationship with food. I could not in good conscience move forward with clients and holistic health with this one last issue unresolved. I had tried restricting, depriving, and dieting to control my eating, but none of those methods worked for long. The steps of Overeaters Anonymous didn't transfer either. This played out much less extremely than in my younger days but manifested itself in weekly sugar and salt binging. Of course, as a holistic health practitioner I maintained eating healthy the rest of the week. With that, I felt like a fraud and I was desperate to end this cycle.

At the time my business was also not profitable. My sincere desire to support others with these life changing practices urged me to bring my business up to par. My dedication and love of sharing these tools led me to The International Association of Wellness Professionals Holistic Wellness Coaching Certification Program (IAWP). I was assured that this would jumpstart my business, and it did just that and much more.

It was here that it all came together. The philosophy of IAWP talked about food in a different way. It wasn't to adhere to this diet or that cleanse. It introduced the concept of eating for energy. This was a new, revolutionary idea called intuitive- or mindful-conscious eating. After six months of receiving coaching, I finally got it. I had been so brainwashed by media and my own negativity into believing that I was never thin enough and that I had no idea what to eat.

When I fully gave myself to this revolutionary approach to eating based on whole foods not laden with chemicals, a world of freedom that I had spent a lifetime searching for opened up before me. No diets, deprivation, or restriction; simply slowing down and listening to my body. Simple and life changing. We'll take a closer look at food and eating in Part III.

The best part of these changes was that I slowly and permanently sloughed off the pounds that had crept up over the years. I lost the weight that I'd put on with menopause gradually, effortlessly, and permanently. More importantly, I stopped fearing food and learned to love food again, foods that gave me lasting energy. Fake foods that I'd once idolized began tasting like a sea of chemicals. I regained the energy I thought I'd never recover. These intuitive eating practices freed me from a lifetime of the insane cycle of diets and disordered eating. Eating the foods that filled me with vibrant energy became the norm. I relaxed with my meals and savored them with great pleasure. Eating became an almost meditative practice in self-love.

As I progressed in my certification classes, I was also trained in something called the CORE Coaching Method™. The IAWP's founder, Suzanne Monroe, explains that the CORE Coaching Method "combines the art of coaching with proven, cutting-edge psychology techniques that address how the brain works in order to help people make lasting changes ... not just about 'changing your habits' for the short-term, instead it's about creating lasting transformations for life by helping you to get to the root of your patterns."

Adding these new tools brought balance quickly to every aspect of my life, including my relationships. My clients also benefited greatly. What a relief for me to not feel that I had to provide all the answers. Now there was a proven formula for accessing one's inner knowing. It was not surprising that with these phenomenal new tools my practice began to thrive. My dreams to reach and offer a truly holistic program delivering sustainable results to both women and men ready for a new kind of change became a reality.

I was thrilled with this approach. This was truly spiritual because by accessing your inner knowing you are accessing divinity, your higher Self. Your higher Self is always right unlike the small self or the ego self. The trick is choosing to tap into and listen to your higher Self.

Eureka! As a holistic practitioner this was a major piece of the puzzle. Along with clearing toxicity at a cellular level and supporting clients with thought and emotional release sessions, I could serve more effectively by ushering them back to the wisdom within. It felt as if the last two puzzle pieces fell into place!

With my brand-new relationship with food, more harmony in my relationships, the shifting of negative thinking, emotional release practices, and removing cellular toxicity through the marvels of bioenergetic testing, I felt invincible! Now, with integrity I could truly empower my clients. The tapestry for a life-transforming series was coming to fruition.

# Chapter 17: Confirmation

"Knowledge is power because it is certain, and certainty is strength. Perception is temporary."

- *A Course in Miracles*

It was on a return trip to Sedona, Arizona that my husband and I were listening to a Pema Chödrön audio entitled "Getting Unstuck" when it hit me. I started writing in the car an article called "Anything but the Present Moment." This was inspired writing. I knew full well that these were not my words. Pema went on in her audio and spoke of staying with the discomfort that sometimes surfaces during meditation. She explained habitual escapism and how it blocks us from spiritual healing by allowing distractions to keep us from diving into our personal barriers. This included escaping into fantasies and one's "to do" list while meditating. I was fully inspired.

Just as I had been practicing for years, I continued to spend my mornings in meditation. However, now during my practice I felt inclined to place pen and paper nearby. Strangely, with my non-dominant left hand, I would scribe ideas coming to me. Divine ideas and words coursed through me. Other writings followed. Articles regarding the barriers to peace poured through me. It all came together when I realized this scribing, along with the author's I had been studying, were all saying the same thing: All answers are within.

Soon after, I was encouraged by a friend to have a psychic reading done by someone she highly recommended. At my reading, the woman opened with, "Your angels are screaming for you to get this out into the world." I hadn't even told her that I had been scribing during meditation. She went on to say, "You are creating a bridge for these higher concepts to share with the world." It dawned on me that I had suspected, but was afraid to admit, I really did have something of value to offer. Perhaps I really could help to empower others. The reading inspired me to write more articles and to form workshops, retreats, and private programs based on these concepts. I called it the Higher Self Care series.

# Part III: Your Task

# Chapter 18: The Wisdom Within

"Deep within you is everything that is perfect, ready to radiate through you and out into the world."

- *A Course in Miracles*

You are already perfect, whole and complete, just as you are. I know this with absolute certainty. When the nows become uncomfortable, it takes courage to dive into them rather than escaping again into quick fixes such as food, shopping, or media. This is the choice you make in the moment. "Do I want to stay stuck or do I want to evolve my life?"

My perceptions of my childhood, my lack of forgiveness, my addictive behaviors, my guilt, and my fears were huge barriers in my life. Miraculously, all of the past dysfunction was aligning with a higher plane. What was not the truth of who I really was fell away like dust in the wind. I was free to become and do what I was led to by the tremendous healing that was taking place in my life.

I discovered that my health problems could be solved by tapping into my meridian system. My desperation spurred me to find solutions that didn't require medications that caused unbearable side effects. I learned to trust my body's innate wisdom, which isn't trusting the body per se but rather trusting the universal love and light that courses through it. This is accessing your higher Self.

Aside from energy reversals, which can be mitigated before testing, I can trust the bioenergetic screening process implicitly. Designed specifically to tap into and measure the subtle energies that flow through the body, this space age technology accurately locates and corrects the source of vital energy imbalance. It detects harmful agents impacting the body's natural healing capabilities. This takes the guesswork out of matching a person's energy field with the most gentle and effective remedies, yielding remarkable results. Years of practicing bioenergetic testing for myself, my family and thousands of clients proved to me that if we directly ask the innate wisdom within it will usher us toward healing every time.

Access your intuition, identify your barriers, dive in, and let go. This brings inner peace and calm naturally. Diving into thoughts, emotions, life imbalance, and even pain are all parts of a working formula that I lovingly call the *Five Steps to Higher Self Care.* It is said that we learn best by doing. Consider delving further by participating in the exercises that follow, bringing these life-changing concepts to a more personal level.

# Chapter 19: Who Am I?

"Your task is not to seek for love, but merely to seek and find all of the barriers within yourself that you have built against it."

– *A Course in Miracles*

You are already the love, light, peace, and better health that you are seeking.

No matter your childhood, illnesses, anxiety, depression, diagnosis, self-doubt, your experiences up to now, your mistakes, your tendency toward habitual escapism, success, failures, wants or desires.

From the cells in your body to the food you ingest, to the relationships in your life, to the emotional baggage you may carry and the onslaught of cyclical thinking that takes up space in your head to your connection with Spirit, these five steps encompass all.

That connection may seem so far away at times. I know for certain the loving guidance within you is just as strong as ever and only a heartbeat away.

Your only task is to release your individual obstacles to peace, one at a time.

All your willingness and courage have paid off. When you know for certain that you can utilize every obstacle in front of you toward your highest good, that you have an expert Guide, and you are bound to grow and become the best you can be almost effortlessly, this is precisely when your personal journey of self-growth becomes fun and becomes exhilarating!

Yes, I mean fun! It becomes an adventure in self-discovery. What's your biggest challenge right now? Hidden in the problem is the key to remembering your way back home.

Yes, I did it the hard way but you don't have to. I am grateful for the privilege to serve those who are ready for change because I can share from personal experience the tools to peace and help you to tap into your innate knowing. I can act as a catalyst to remembering your sense of joy, of love, and of beauty. This inner calm surpasses anything you've ever experienced and transcends the world of chaos.

I have had the privilege of leading others through fear and pain and out to the other side to discover the wisdom within. And in this process, reinforcing their spiritual resilience and empowering them to extend their love, live with passion, and fulfill their unique purpose unfettered.

Imagine a state of mind that focuses only on this instant, laced with rich opportunity to align with your inner knowing. Imagine a world where you are not forcing every action but are moved from within to act through sheer inspiration. A world beyond seeming chaos where you know you are safe and loved beyond your wildest dreams. Imagine a world where fearing your emotions is a thing of the past. Imagine a world where there is no lack and you receive and give love to everyone, unconstrained by wavering self-worth or the propensity to judge others. Where you can walk freely with complete peace of mind.

What if outside the NOW nothing is real? What if you awakened and were no longer drawn off course by the dramas in this realm? There you would experience no fear, no insecurity and no lack. It starts with your courage and willingness.

"Heaven is not a place nor a condition. It is merely an awareness of perfect Oneness and the knowledge that there is nothing else; nothing outside this Oneness and nothing else within."

- *A Course in Miracles*

Many years ago, my 3-year-old grandson, Jesiah, asked me a profound question. Just a moment before, I had shared with him that I met with a client that day who happened to be his preschool teacher. I shouted out to him with great enthusiasm, "She knows who you are!" He looked up from his play quizzically and said, "Who am I?" I laughed so hard I was crying.

It takes great support to look beyond the identity we assume on Earth. How do we separate who we are with what we do? Our whole lives are geared toward doing and becoming more. How we look. How smart we are. Our relationship to gravity. How much money we generate. Even our state of physical health seems to define us while walking this Earth. We simply can't win competing against ourselves to become something we are not. The bottom line is that inner peace lies in the knowledge that you are perfect, whole and complete just as you are. You need not look outside yourself. You need do nothing to prove your completeness. Therein lies peace and happiness.

## *NOTES*

# *NOTES*

# Chapter 20: Evolving is Essential

"It is not necessary to seek for what is true, but it *is* necessary to seek for what is false. Every illusion is one of fear, whatever form it takes. And the attempt to escape from one illusion into another must fail. If you seek love outside yourself you can be certain that you perceive hatred within, and are afraid of it. Yet peace will never come from the illusion of love, but only from its reality."

- *A Course in Miracles*

A bit of ancient wisdom from a Sufi proverb: "You are in earth school. You are here to learn lessons. You may like the lessons or choose to ignore them. No matter, a lesson is repeated in various forms until learned." The message portrayed in my mind is a basic need, like food and water equates to inner growth. Evolving spiritually is not an option. It is essential.

I can choose to fight what shows up in my life, or I can choose to embrace it. When I'm listening to ego thoughts, not consciously aware, I tend to resist every change or lesson that comes my way. That may include positive changes too. My small egoic mind wants to keep me stagnate and trapped in a box. It wants to keep me as far away from the answers within as possible. Why? Because the presence of higher wisdom dissolves ego.

On the other hand, when I choose to remain awake, I can first embrace the resistance and grow from there. Secondly, I can choose to meet whatever is coming down the pike head on, my next earth school assignment, with open arms.

This requires a remembering. It is when I awaken to my ever-present connection to my inner Guide, my Source, God if you will, that it allows for this remembering to occur.

## Step One: Access Your Intuition

ASK YOURSELF: What brings you back to center? What fortifies your faith in the ultimate good? Is it a discipline, an activity, a person, place or thing? Whatever it is, embrace and nurture it!

Many that I've spoken to about connecting with their divine oneness have no doubt about what brings them to this peace. They are eager to share. Though their answers vary to some degree, most reveal practices or activities such as: meditation, prayer, being in nature, listening to music, artistic or creative pursuits, dance, slowing down enough to smell the roses, spending time with a beloved pet, and experiencing the innocence of children. Unconditional love seems to be the common thread with the latter two examples.

While steeped in these practices, the memories of the love and beauty that are always there come bubbling to the surface. Yes, this is spirit – the fire inside each of us that allows the light within to shine through.

How can you grow this peace and oneness inside you? Whatever it is for you, explore and fortify it daily if possible. It only takes a moment in most cases, just an instance of embracing this moment fully. Now is where the miracle of oneness is found.

Suppose, in the moment, you're filled with insurmountable barriers to peace and you find yourself unwilling to choose differently. You have decided, like a truck spinning its wheels, to remain stuck in the muck. What if your present moment truly seems awful? Well, in my experience, while fully awake, I simply see this as another lesson and take the next step to welcome even the so-called muck as best I can. It is through the process of diving into the muck in the moment that it is transformed.

If accessing the spirit within was the whole story, wouldn't we be living in bliss? Enter the realm of digging deeper into your current obstacles to bliss.

WHAT IS BLOCKING YOU? Before we go into the second step, a word about your personal obstacles to peace: Barriers can range from thoughts, emotions and navigating life on earth.

Like a thick brick wall, cyclical negative thinking can be an enormous barrier. I liken thoughts to the element of air. They are constantly blowing through our heads.

Barriers can also show up as feeling blindsided by a constant torrent of overwhelming emotion. Emotion is energy in motion. It is often the unpleasant result of cyclical thinking. Like water it is meant to flow. It's when we damn the flow of emotion that it can show up in explosive outbursts or implosive health issues.

I have found that navigating the physical world, which I liken to the element of earth, can also derail us from our divine connection. This includes juggling our careers, finances, relationships, households and the care and feeding of our bodies; food, water, fresh air, sleep and exercise. Did I miss anything?

Each of these three aforementioned obstacles have a deliberate purpose. They serve to distract us from our intuitive knowing. This is the ego's playground. Why does the ego love long "to-do" lists and problems? Because they only serve to keep us nonplussed and effectively block our connection to our intuition.

What if you reframe these perceived barriers as lessons? The iconic author Norman Vincent Peale states that "within every problem is the solution." Suppose our convoluted problems are just an earth lesson meant to bring us back to joy, peace and love.

In the pages to come you will discover straightforward techniques for doing just that.

## Step Two: Identify the Barriers

Step two begins by identifying which category the current problem is in. Personally, I must ask for a little help here, because my knee-jerk reaction to any problem is to suppress, push away or procrastinate by opening the refrigerator, somehow expecting food to ease anxiety. Surprisingly, exactly this crept up during the editing process of my first book. I find this interesting as I had successfully abandoned this habit years before.

Identification can be tricky. You see, the ego/small self will use thoughts that elicit fear or self-righteousness to keep you in chains. It will produce thoughts such as "This is too scary or risky" or that you should "Avoid dealing with this at all costs." It will go on to suggest things like, "…besides, doesn't that dessert look tempting? And don't I deserve it" or "Why not spend hours online to research and buy that item you've been wanting for so long? You can deal with the consequences later."

These thoughts are distracting you from that which would heighten the realization of your worth and self-love. It is so much cleaner when you can reward yourself from a place of higher self-care and not blindly be lured by the all too seductive mind chatter in your head.

Is your biggest obstacle in the realm of thought or emotion, or is it physical, such as food confusion, an ailment or chronic busyness?

## Step Three: Dive Into the Interference

Once the barrier is identified, choose to dive into it. Dive into it with conscious attention and curiosity. Yes, this may take courage. It is so tempting to do the pushing away that you've always done. Remember that the courage to persevere is generously offered by your inner teacher. The Teacher within is with you every step of the way.

Dare to dive into the interference. This is achieved by examining the thought, experiencing the emotion, or exploring the area of physical imbalance. As hair-raising as it may sound right now, when you fully dive into it, usually only five minutes are needed to shift your entire outlook.

> "I went to Donna Lee to help with clearing thinking that impacted my life in a negative way, including the inability to process emotion. She helped me set goals to restructure my entire life. She worked with me on

what was important to me. Now looking back, through her nurturing guidance, we accomplished so much more than I ever realized.

As we addressed topics that arose and worked on releasing emotions that were layered and disguised as other emotions, the process almost seemed magical that these sentiments would disappear or have less impact on the way they ruled my life.

Surprisingly though it didn't stop there. I discovered Pandora's box beneath surfacing emotions. What I had hidden away and ignored began to come out. I originally started with the little things. I then, realized that I was my own worst enemy.

It was hard to face. This time though, I had the tools and guidance to work through my Pandora's box. I wasn't dependent on anyone's advice to lean on, although it is nice and available if needed. My success through the Higher Self Care Program was due to tapping into my own inner knowing. I don't recommend working with Donna Lee if you enjoy staying stuck with what haunts you. She can help give you the drive to work through difficult emotions to something better. Facing our own demons is difficult but coming out the other side is incredible!"

– Tammy A.

## Step Four: Let Go of What's Blocking You

The thought that had you paralyzed a moment before can seem almost laughable. It can then be reframed to a more loving and truer thought which elevates you rather than defeats you.

The emotion literally begins to dissolve while diving into it. According to St. Paul, what you bring to the light of consciousness becomes the light. The uncomfortable emotion dissolves and is released and you pop up into your true nature of authentic peace and calm. The peace that was there all along. You find you don't have to try to think positively to feel happier, it just happens organically.

I like to share a story of my good friend and colleague, Laura. As a practitioner she was well aware of the oppressive thoughts and emotions she had been experiencing for ages. She decided to take the direct approach to inner peace.

She began by walking in nature, meditating by a creek, petting her dog and doing some yoga. On the drive home she listened to some soothing music. However, anxiety, worry, anger and frustration surfaced with a vengeance as her thoughts went to world events and the neighbor who had angered her the day before.

"Where is peace?" she screamed. "I simply cannot live my life in lotus position." It occurred to Laura that perhaps peace could be found at the mall or by shopping online. Suddenly, she was convinced that it was in that carton of ice cream in the fridge. No not here. It's got to be in the bag of chips in the pantry. Disappointed again she went back to her computer, pulled out her credit card, booked a vacation, and played the stock market. She weighed herself on the bathroom scale – peace definitely wasn't there. She poured a glass of wine and then a second. Still no luck.

More determined than ever, she pushed on with her quest. "Of course!" she exclaimed, "if my family was happy then I could have peace." Unfortunately, she quickly found you cannot MAKE others happy. Have you ever tried? Exhausted at this point, walking around in pants that were too tight, broke, tipsy and sobbing, Laura nearly gave up.

The trouble is we can get lost for years in the cycle of our pursuit for peace. She was experiencing first-hand what Pema Chödrön calls "habitual escapism"; going for the short-lived quick fixes which lead to more misery instead of the tranquility one is seeking. As it happens, it is not by skirting around what is currently disturbing you, but rather it is by welcoming the very thing that seems to be robbing you of peace.

I have always admired Laura's sheer determination. Little did she know her frantic search was taking her further away from her goal. She then took a step back and did something radical. She slowed down. She identified and isolated the one most disturbing thought in her head. She dove into that belief instead of the Oreos. Suddenly, the thought that had her hostage a moment before seemed absolutely ludicrous. It was just a thought!

That's when she discovered it. In that very ordinary moment. She gave herself fully to the heavy emotions she was experiencing. It was a dark place, empty, like a great void within. Trembling she dared go deeper. Within two minutes the depression totally and completely lifted. The peace she was seeking was inside all along!

The essence of you is perfect peace. No thought you can think, no emotion you can feel, no circumstance in your life can change that.

Suppose your biggest current obstacle is your physical existence on earth, such as your to-do list, career, or relationships. Suddenly, after several minutes of diving into the area you'd identified as imbalanced, you have an intuitive thought that seems to come out of nowhere. Why hadn't you thought of this before? It was blocked by the static in the busyness of your daily existence. Now it's clear to you what to do to rebalance this area of your life. It's so simple. And you'll find that the inspired next step is usually a small doable action that often excites you. You find as soon as you act on this inspired thought that life balance is once again achieved.

## Step Five: Experience Authentic Joy

What just happened? You just embraced your personal earth school lesson with your eyes wide open. Now you are back! You have succeeded in raising your vibration. You've taken a giant spiritual step in just five minutes. You've loosened the chains. You're living with more freedom! You may laugh at your old habit of sidestepping your perceived problems.

You have evolved beyond egoic thinking and have opened a tiny crack to revealing the truth of who you are and always were. As noted earlier, just like food and water is essential while on earth, so is spiritual growth. You are here to learn lessons. The lessons that bring you back to your perfect innocence, your infallibility, and the thread that links you to your immortality.

Congratulations!

## "RULES FOR BEING HUMAN"

an Ancient Sufi Proverb

YOU WILL RECEIVE A BODY
You may like it or hate it, the choice is yours,
but it will be yours for the entire period this time around.

YOU WILL LEARN LESSONS

You are enrolled in a full-time school called life.
Each day in this school you will have the opportunity to learn lessons.
You may like the lessons or think of them as irrelevant and hence choose to ignore them.
No matter, keep reading.

A LESSON IS REPEATED UNTIL LEARNED

A lesson will be presented to you in various forms until you have learned it.
When you have learned it, you can go on to the next lesson.

THERE ARE NO SINS, ONLY MISTAKES CALLING FOR CORRECTION

Growth is a process of trial and error; experimentation.
The "failed" experiment is as much a part of the process as the experiment that actually "works".

LEARNING LESSONS DOES NOT END

There is no part of life that does not contain lessons.
If you are alive, there are lessons to be learned.

THERE.... IS NO BETTER THAN....HERE

When your "there" becomes a "here", you will simply obtain another "there" that will again look better than "here".

OTHERS ARE MERELY MIRRORS OF YOU
You cannot love or hate something about another person unless it reflects to you something you love or hate about yourself.

YOUR ANSWERS LIE ONLY INSIDE YOU
The answer to life's questions lie only inside you. All you need to do is look, listen, and trust.

YOU WILL FORGET ALL OF THIS!

Yes, you will forget, guaranteed. I promise this is a practice in remembering. Each time you choose to courageously embrace perceived problems as suggested in the Five Steps, you will be brought back to the wisdom within you beyond the vicissitudes of this ego-dominated world.

Join me as we journey together through the Five Steps back to enlightenment to uncover what is blocking your peace. Together we shall discover your way back to perfect joy.

It is my passion and sincere privilege to share these life changing secrets with those of you who desire growth.

# *NOTES*

# *NOTES*

# *NOTES*

# Chapter 21: The Solution

"There is an ancient peace you carry in your heart and have not lost."

- *A Course in Miracles*

The old paradigm just doesn't work anymore, keeping us stuck, flabby, frazzled and fatigued. The new paradigm is courageously diving into life's ups and downs. Looking for our center outside ourselves only leads to frustration. Real joy is not in the next vacation, pay raise, dessert or glass of wine. In our society we are bombarded with the next fix outside of ourselves – the next supplement, tincture, book, fad diet or cleanse. Consider the media and how the next life-changing product is just around the corner.

"You have so little faith in yourself because you are unwilling to accept the fact that perfect love is in you, and so you seek without for what you cannot find within."

- *A Course in Miracles*

## Five Steps to Higher Self Care

1. Access Your Intuition
2. Identify the Barriers
3. Dive Into the Interference
4. Let Go of the Blockages
5. Experience Authentic Joy

### #1 – ACCESS YOUR INTUITION

"Connecting to your Higher Self is really the most natural thing we can do."

- *A Course in Miracles*

We must know where authentic joy is before we can achieve it. As noted previously in the "Rules for Being Human," the answers to life's questions lie only inside you. All you need do is look, listen and trust.

What brings you instant peace? My purpose and privilege is to provide a beacon for you to reach peace more certainly. Intuition is defined as a thing that one knows or considers, likely from instinctive feeling rather than conscious reasoning.

It is important to note here that the conscious reasoning is again the realm of ego. Intuition and inner peace are likened to the element of fire. It is connecting with our spirit, our Source, our inner guidance. It is the spark of inspiration within that never goes out.

Examples of connection, as previously stated: nature, exercise and movement, music, art, pouring oneself into a project, yoga, meditation, enjoying pets, experiencing the innocence of a baby. What two attributes do these activities have in common? Number one, they are sourced from within and secondly, they occur in a specific timeline – now.

Yet, we find ourselves turning away from the present consistently. Why? What are we so afraid of? I have found that allowing and giving myself fully to what is here now is the only way through. This is always true, except when physical harm is imminent. Even in the case of danger, the next right action is accessed in the now, so of course you will know to remove yourself. The truth of who we are is found only in the now. When we surrender fully to this moment unconditionally it is then that we discover our higher, intuitive, whole, complete Self.

Remember my example of embracing ordinary moments to relieve a bad habit? Ordinary moments are designed for those of you who cannot fit in meditation, yoga or walks in nature.

I encourage you in the following "dig deeper" exercise and the exercises throughout the remainder of this book to explore each that pertains to you. Participating in the suggested activities may serve to jumpstart your spiritual journey. If so inspired, take it a step further by journaling about any ideas or insights that came up during the exercises. As stated earlier, we learn best by doing. However, adding writing to the process can help to organize ideas and can be therapeutic, as well as giving a fresh new self-perspective.

> Dig deeper:
>
> The body can be utilized for accessing the present. Set a timer for five minutes and sink into the moment.
>
> Become aware of your inner sensations and outer surroundings – what you are hearing, seeing, smelling, tasting, feeling, and sensing right now.
>
> If you are fully giving yourself to this simple practice, by the time your timer goes off you will experience ineffable peace.

So what's the catch? Why aren't we peaceful if it's that simple?

The catch: We are bombarded with distractions that block our peace, purpose and potential.

## #2 – IDENTIFY THE BARRIERS

"As peace extends from deep inside yourself to embrace all the Sonship and give it rest, it will encounter many obstacles."

- *A Course in Miracles*

Dig deeper:

Take out a sheet of paper. Jot down what typically pulls you out of a state of calm or joy:

__________________________________________

__________________________________________

Does it have to do with attending to the demands of the physical world we live in, a disturbing thought, or perhaps an unsettling feeling?

Again, in my experience I have found there are three major blocks to peace. Negative or egoic cyclical thinking, emotional overwhelm and navigating the physical world such as imbalance in health issues, juggling daily tasks, or in the care and feeding of the body.

Most of our barriers originate in our thinking which in turn activates emotions. When our thinking and emotions are discordant, our bodies follow suit which results in fatigue and a propensity toward life imbalance, leading to interpersonal strife, injury or illness.

It bears repeating: The truth of who you are is perfect love and light. The essence that is you is perfect, whole and complete in spite of perceived barriers. The truth of who you are is beyond any thought you can think, any emotion you can feel or any physical imbalance you can experience.

Barriers can be a hidden opportunity. We can utilize our personal barriers as a welcomed springboard toward inner growth. Your obstacles in life are your roadmap back home to your peaceful, joyful, intuitive, secure higher Self.

## #3 – DIVE IN

"Your part is only to offer Him a little willingness to let Him remove all fear and hatred, and to be forgiven."

- *A Course in Miracles*

Until we embrace what's blocking us, we will remain feeling disconnected, isolated and alone. Laura, after much procrastination, dove into her biggest obstacle by examining her thought and experiencing her emotion. This was not easy, much like diving into ice cold water, but she came out refreshed and lighter beyond her imaginings. In my mind, this is the step that requires the most courage.

Diving in can be broken down into the three E's: Examine the thought. Experience the emotion. Explore the area of life imbalance.

> Dig deeper:
>
> In the previous exercise you identified an area that pulls you out of calm. A thought, emotion or imbalance in your physical world. Now allow yourself to take just 90 seconds – if it's a thought, jot it down and note if it's a fact or opinion.
>
> If it's an emotion, name it and sink into the vibration of emotion with curiosity.
>
> If it's an area of physical imbalance, ask the wisdom within to reveal an action that you could implement that might bring balance. Note what you discover.

It is by diving into your barriers that you build and strengthen your intuition, your connection to Source. This step, however, can be daunting for most of us. Who wants to examine negative thoughts or dive into emotion or take necessary action to rebalance their daily existence? With expert support, the act of diving in becomes second nature.

## #4 – LET GO

"Now you must learn that only infinite patience produces immediate effects. This is the way in which time is exchanged for eternity. Infinite patience calls upon infinite love, and by producing results *now* it renders time unnecessary."

- *A Course in Miracles*

Now that you've identified and become willing to dive in, you can let go. When my colleague Laura allowed herself to experience her emotions in her dynamic search for peace, the act of letting go happened almost without effort on her part. As she stayed with the feelings of anxiety and anger, she felt an immediate relief, a lightening of spirit. She had truly let go.

This is the simple process of what I refer to as the three R's: Reframing the thought. Releasing the emotion. Rebalancing your life.

Dig deeper:

Refer again to what pulls you out of a calm state that you jotted down from the previous exercise. Stay with the thought, emotion or physical imbalance by breathing into it with curiosity and letting go of the outcome.

> You identified it, you dove into it, now can you let it go?
>
> Don't be surprised if it let go of its own accord when you surrendered to the diving in process. You'll know if you've succeeded if you feel relieved, lighter, or excited.

## STEP #5 – EXPERIENCE AUTHENTIC JOY

"All healing is essentially the release from fear."

- *A Course in Miracles*

You don't actually take this step. Your higher Self does. It happens automatically as you work through steps two through four. It occurs naturally when you let go of all that blocks your serenity.

You will experience a sense of calm and joy that outshines anything that you imagined. Not only that, but you will have sudden clarity. You naturally become filled with passion and a certain purpose. You are in that instant plugged into your intuition.

Yes, you are in earth school, and as long as you are wandering this earth, you'll continue to encounter problems. This is the good news because each perceived problem in your life can be used to expedite your journey back home. The beauty is you can start at step one and repeat these steps as needed.

*NOTES*

# *NOTES*

# Chapter 22: Wind, Rain and Mud

I was conducting a higher self-care workshop at a yoga studio several years ago, and as I drew my usual diagram on the board, the elements of fire, air, water and earth revealed themselves.

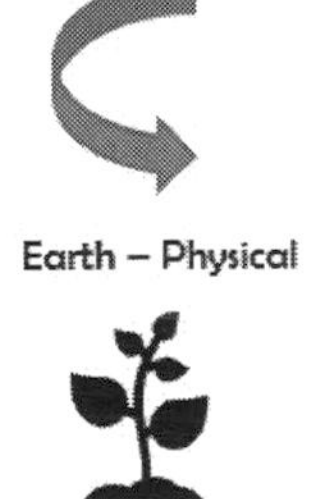

Fire is the light of inspiration within that never goes out, and the three barriers to peace lined up; thoughts pass through our heads like clouds in the sky, emotions like water are meant to flow, and earth represents the navigating of the physical world in which we reside. Each of the latter three elements can pull us away from the light within, but as shown in the diagram, it is by diving into the outer elements that we miraculously come back to our center, the fiery brilliance within.

Clients report that differentiating by visualizing a particular element with the three barriers really helps to grasp these concepts. It seems that identifying their most pressing barrier becomes simpler when they can correlate it with natural phenomena. Afterall, we are blown away by our thoughts, represented by the element of air; we can drown in our emotions, represented by water; we walk on the earth, which represents the physical barrier; and of course the central piece, the flame within, is our eternal connection to Source.

## A Closer Look at Air: Thoughts

You will know that cyclical thinking has you in its throes if you experience obsessive thinking, negative mind chatter, insults toward yourself or others, feelings of inferiority or superiority, second thoughts, self-doubt, uncertainty or feeling mentally paralyzed.

Fact or Fiction?

Repetitive thoughts are made up of stories we tell ourselves based on old beliefs and assumptions, leaving no room in our lives for divine guidance. Why torture ourselves with untruths when we are capable of reframing them? How many times have we drifted from the perfect innocence and beauty of the present moment due to the lure of cyclical thinking? My worst enemy, quite possibly, lives inside my head.

Eckhart Tolle goes so far as to say we are "addicted to thinking." We are not our thoughts, and just because we heard it in our head doesn't make it true. Like you, I have wasted valuable hours obsessing about the past which is gone and the future which may never happen.

Through much study and practice I have acquired tools and techniques which effectively pull me out of this ongoing madness. Am I suggesting that we are mad? No, but our thoughts can be. Believing these thoughts only serves to perpetuate them. Examining an old thought or belief is the beginning of transcending it. And yes, it requires willingness, discipline, and commitment.

- Most thoughts are recycled old beliefs and assumptions.
- Identifying a thought is the first step to transcending it.

- We can learn to let go of thoughts and free ourselves instantly.

Empower yourself by taking a moment to **really look** at what you are thinking. Only then can you truly let it go and reconnect with your authentic self. This "taking a moment to look" interrupts the pattern and brings us back to the truth of who we are.

Practice Disbelieving

"What you perceive in others you are strengthening in yourself."

- *A Course in Miracles*

We are not meant to be controlled by distorted stories that elicit depression, worriment, or anger. This all-consuming saga only serves to distract us from the wonder and joy in our lives now.

We are now tapping into the realm of peace. This couldn't be more apparent than in our interpersonal relationships. The small mind must keep us in turmoil and finds fertile ground in our communications with coworkers, friends and family. When we lean on ego advice, it can throw a wrench into what may otherwise be a loving and kind exchange.

"But it's his/her fault!" Blaming others keeps us stuck. This gets us nowhere on our path to growth. Plus, it takes away our power. We give another person the power to control us. This is just another diversion from our lessons toward oneness.

## A Closer Look at Water: Emotions

You will recognize the barrier of unprocessed emotion if you experience these symptoms: endless crying or complaining, lashing out at others, feeling apathetic or depressed, incessant anxiety or worry, feeling out of control.

This includes lusting, yearning for more. You will find as you read further that it's just another emotion, not good or bad. However, unconscious lingering in emotional yearning can contribute to staying stuck.

Yes, of course we will continue to experience these thoughts and emotions, but they become like leaves drifting down a river as they pass through. Feel the feelings and discard the assumptions. Peace finds you, and intuitive thought creeps in.

You check inside and may instinctively know to go right instead of left. Now, you are guided by the connection of your true Source, no longer being pulled into perpetual madness. You begin to feel more centered and have a certainty that transcends the lure of any old story circulating in your head.

## A Closer Look at Earth: Navigating the Physical World

Do you experience the following symptoms? Lowered immunity, prone to injuries or ill health, caffeine or sugar addiction, over- or under-eating, chronic busyness, fatigue, inexplicable symptoms, career confusion, financial struggles, reduced efficiency at home or work, or strained relationships. If so, you are experiencing physical world barriers.

"If he/she/they would just change." This is another egoic pitfall that keeps us stuck. Wanting to change or fix another takes the focus off of us which keeps us stuck in the old paradigm. Besides, do you have the power to change another? How would you react if someone in your life wanted to "fix you"? This is clearly a recipe for interpersonal disaster.

### Does This Mean We're Skewed?

Most thoughts are recycled old beliefs and assumptions. Believing these thoughts only serves to perpetuate them. Identifying a thought is the first step to transcending it. We can learn to let go of thoughts and free ourselves instantly.

Thoughts are like clouds, likened to the element of air. As author Byron Katie puts it, "It's not the thought passing through our mind, it's when we become attached to it that it becomes a problem."

Do we really see things through our own personal filter: skewing the truth? Have you ever witnessed an accident and learned that the person across the street saw it in a completely different way? Or a good friend was miffed about something you said, but what you intended and what was heard was opposite, to say the least? Perhaps your aunt tells a story that your mother recalls quite differently? How could this be?

As we emerge into this world, we are provided with an adequate temporary suit that we call a body, a product of ego. It usually comes with five senses or filters. The ego, or small self, is very uncomfortable with the enigmatic and cannot survive in the light of the present moment. If the ego becomes threatened, it will make up stories by accessing the past or imagining the future. These fictional egoic thoughts will cloud your perceptions and cause emotions to surface, namely fear, and inevitably keep you stuck.

Albert Einstein states, "The most beautiful thing we can experience is the mysterious. It is the source of all true art and science."

Stories colored by the only reference ego has, the past or the future, flood into the mystery. Jumping to conclusions and making assumptions purely based on past or future bring unnecessary stress. Talk about clouding our perceptions! It's not the event but our view of the event that causes stress, as observed by Epictetus: "It is our attitude toward events, not events themselves, which we can control. Nothing is by its own nature calamitous – even death is terrible only if we fear it."

- Perception is skewed as it comes through our physical senses.
- We are not just bodies. We are so much more; above and beyond anything a body can experience.
- We can learn simple techniques to clear our perceptions and experience peace.
- Just *being in the now* rather than *doing*, which is the ego's domain, releases us.

Remember the scene in the 2009 film *Avatar* when the heroine says, "I SEE YOU!" She is seeing beyond the filter. That is higher vision. Look for the light of innocence in others because that's the truth of who you are and who they are. Even though appearances may seem otherwise, we can learn to focus beyond our perceptions to the certainty of higher vision.

# *NOTES*

*NOTES*

# Chapter 23: Reframing Thought

"When you meet anyone, remember it is a holy encounter. As you see him you will see yourself, as you think of him you will think of yourself. Never forget this for in him you will find yourself or lose yourself."

- *A Course in Miracles*

What were you thinking?

When you dissect individual thoughts, you find that often what you are thinking isn't even accurate. When you see what it is you're really thinking and realize it isn't true, quite often the opposite is true. You are beginning to free yourself.

As previously stated, "Thoughts are just passing through the sky of our minds." If you've ever meditated, thoughts come and go. Meditation is a process of allowing thoughts to drift through. However, the temptation to latch on to thought can take you away from the bulk of your meditation time. Even after forty years it's not uncommon for me to get lost in thought and not realize it until meditation time is over.

Consider these encouraging words from the American Tibetan Buddhist, Pema Chödrön:

> "After a time, the flood of thoughts will start to slow down and you will start to feel a relief and a peacefulness and even a relaxation in the body from not getting caught up with them. You will find that you can then prolong this thought free state for longer periods. The next time you sit to meditate it will be easier to maintain. Then even when not sitting in formal meditation, in your normal everyday life, you will find yourself starting to enjoy not getting involved in the many countless thoughts. It gives you a wonderful sense of freedom. And it enables you to start observing how others are dictated to by their ever-chattering minds. If you can stay centered in this self it gives you a calmness, a sense of peace and ultimately a feeling of bliss."

Ego lives on assumptions and opinions. Most of our thoughts are governed by ego. Ego knows nothing and can only make up stories about what it thinks is true. However, the realm of all-knowing spirit, intuition, inspiration, peace, joy, love and inner calm are your natural state. When you are tapped into Spirit, and the strife and struggle dissolve, you will instead feel moved or inspired to take an action. This is quite often felt as a sort of quickening in the solar plexus, as many clients have shared.

Are these facts or opinions? Thoughts such as "I'm not good enough," "I'm stupid, I'm fat, I'm ugly," and "I'm not smart enough" only cause unnecessary suffering and do nothing to inspire change. The realm of spirit knows. Ego guesses.

The space of not knowing is the realm of joy, inner calm and peace. The gaps between the thoughts in our heads is where inner peace is found.

> Dig deeper:
>
> As the Sufi Proverb cited earlier, others are mirrors of your perception of yourself. Consider a glaring defect in someone you know.
>
> Now take a moment to see where you have judged yourself as having this very same defect but tucked it away in your subconscious.

The disowning of a past bad habit acts like a burr under the saddle of our subconscious. It is because our small self is a master of pushing our defects out of our minds. We automatically project it outward, thinking this will get rid of it, and then recognize it blatantly in another. Hence, it irritates us even more so when we see it playing out in another's behavior.

Examining thoughts can serve to literally clear the air in most relationships. Jody participated in a workshop that I led. She was struggling with anger toward a former roommate and friend who owed her money. She volunteered to assist me in demonstrating the exercise. She shared her angry story of how a roommate and supposed friend left her high and dry with three months back rent. She had been nursing this resentment for eight months. Together we demonstrated the formula for changing thoughts. After she identified the underlying thought and reframed it, she was still discouraged, and on the way out mentioned how this exercise really didn't do anything for her. To my amazement she called me the next day. Ecstatic, she reported that she had received the money in full that very morning. Proof that when you shift your thoughts your world shifts.

Dig deeper:

Identify your most disturbing thought. Write it down. You may notice a feeling of resistance. This is the ego fighting the process.

Dive into that sentence. Ask yourself "Is this a fact or an opinion"? Be honest with yourself. Is this one thought hurting the other or is it just causing you inner turmoil?

Reframe it by rewording it to reflect fact only. It may surprise you how much kinder, shorter and simpler your new sentence is.

Enjoy the miraculous relief of a complete shift in perception.

"...Peace of mind is clearly an internal matter. It must begin with your own thoughts, and then extend outward."

- *A Course in Miracles*

It's true. We do need ego thinking to balance our check books, but we don't have to live there. Ego can be associated with the left brain that does analytical things such as reading, writing and arithmetic. It's needed while we're navigating the physical world.

# *NOTES*

# *NOTES*

# *NOTES*

# Chapter 24: Releasing Emotion

"I have said you have but two emotions, love and fear. One is changeless but continually exchanged, being offered by the eternal to the eternal."

– *A Course in Miracles*

Emotions are likened to the element of Water. Emotions are meant to flow.

When we damn up or suppress our emotions, they tend to come out sideways, verbally attacking others, crying uncontrollably, slamming the door, irritability or feeling sorry for ourselves. Thoughts breed emotion. It stands to reason that when we attach to a thought, we immediately experience emotion. Often, we are unaware of the thought preceding the emotion. The unchecked thought literally controls our moods, actions and even our health.

Keep in mind that when emotion becomes overwhelming, no amount of dissecting thought will get you through. At that point you must identify and dive into the vibration of emotion, letting go of the story (or the series of thoughts that triggered the emotion) completely. Diving in takes an experienced guide initially and then after much practice you are empowered to employ this technique on your own even while in mid-conversation.

Honor yourself by honoring what you are feeling. This will allow you to become more at ease, more authentic and more you in every area of your life. Nothing to hide; no pretenses, just unadulterated self-acceptance and freedom.

When I became versed in this practice, I began rediscovering me. I would dance, sing, and play like a child at times. Without the old self-censorship that preceded my every word, I began to say exactly what came to me in the moment. Suddenly there was no barrier between me and you. When friends, colleagues and clients would mention that I seemed so authentic, my heart would fill with joy because that was the highest compliment I could ever receive.

When we come into this world as babies, we feel what we feel. Then as we outgrow toddlerhood society, parents and teachers tell us to stifle our feelings, shut up, be quiet, don't cry, and tell your brother you're sorry, even when you are not sorry. In this world we are conditioned to suppress what we feel.

Each emotion has its own vibration like the notes on the piano. The low and high frequencies on a piano create beautiful music. Just as there are no bad notes, there are no bad emotions. Surfacing emotion cannot hurt you though it may seem like it can. It's just different energy or like the variation of notes on a piano. Simply allow yourself to feel what you do for approximately 90 seconds.

Processing emotion is really quite simple. The act of bringing your conscious attention to surfacing emotion will allow it to dissolve. Acknowledging the sensations, with curiosity in your body, with each emotion is the key.

> Dig deeper:
>
> Simply ask "What am I feeling?" Identify it as best you can.
>
> Is it anger, joy, sadness, fear or depression? There are many frequencies of emotion, none worse than the others, just a note on a piano.
>
> At the deepest level every emotion is some aspect of joy!

Having trouble bringing up an emotion?

> Dig deeper:
>
> Sit in front of a mirror and look into your eyes. Within seconds you will begin to feel emotion.
>
> Yes, even boredom, resistance, numbness and indifference are found on the scale of emotion.

Once identified, breathe fully into the feeling and stay with it for at least 90 seconds. It will either lessen, be replaced by another emotion or dissolve entirely.

# *NOTES*

# *NOTES*

# Chapter 25: Rebalancing the Physical

"The Holy Spirit, as always, takes what you have made and translates it into a learning device. Again as always, He reinterprets what the ego uses as an argument for separation into a demonstration against it."

- *A Course in Miracles*

Navigating the physical world is likened to the element of Earth.

This brings us to the third element that blocks the spark and our connection to Source. Physical self-care is foundational. If our everyday lives or our own health are out of balance it will most certainly interfere with our precious opportunities for inner growth. Navigating the physical world that we live in includes life balance, health and food. It consists of what we must do to sustain our daily existence, specifically with regard to a career, finances, relationships, spirituality, mindset, water, food, sleep, exercise and fresh air. It's a full-time job and leaves little time to smell the roses. With all of these areas to keep in balance it's tempting to procrastinate. Another ploy of the ego, as you've probably found, is procrastination, a direct attack on your self-esteem. However, we can also utilize our struggle with daily imbalances to come back to center and a sense of calm.

Dig deeper:

**Identify** one area where you are currently out of balance.

Next, **dive in** by taking a moment to connect with Source. Jot down one to three small steps that might help correct the imbalance.

___________________________________________

___________________________________________

___________________________________________

Finally, choose just one step you'd be willing to do and commit to doing it for the next two weeks. Do your best to **let go** of the results for now.

The key word is willing. If you put down "I should do this" or "shouldn't do that," chances are that you won't do it at all. That's your ego talking.

Pat W., a former client and graduate of the Higher Self Care Program, is a great example of how taking one small step toward self-care can bring balance. She was overwhelmed with daily tasks and couldn't see any way to interrupt this pattern. During one of her sessions in the program she got an insight and decided to take two small action steps. She began by scheduling time for self-care each day. As she shares below, implementing self-care improved her relationships.

"My relationships, particularly with my husband, were not healthy, and I was having feelings of depression because I could not get things balanced in my life and felt like I was moving in circles. I have much more energy as my small action step led to me not only enjoying quiet time and fresh air, but I began eating right and taking care of myself overall.

My life has improved in many areas. My biggest breakthrough: By taking care of myself first, my days seemed to flow better and my relationships greatly improved (especially with my husband)! I now feel much happier and my health has greatly improved."

## A Word About Food

Let's start with the basics: Fueling for Energy. This topic is particularly meaningful to me due to my years of struggle with disordered eating. I could write an entire book on how these revolutionary concepts with regard to food and eating have transformed my life.

Our bodies run best on natural sources, such as whole unprocessed foods.

Processed foods, refined flour, white rice, pasta, sugary items, boxed and packaged foods are, as a rule, chemical-laden fake foods and don't give the body the energy and lasting fuel it needs in the demands of our daily lives. These can affect our moods and our energy levels, not to mention our health, all of which can have a direct impact on your inner peace.

The processed, or fake, foods are recognized within the body as foreign or harmful. When consumed, they are diverted to the liver, which coincidentally produces fat to shield the body from these foreign chemicals and over-abundance of sugars.

What are whole foods? Whole foods are generally those that remain close to their state in nature. They do not have added sugars, preservatives, flavorings, or other manufactured ingredients. They are not produced in a factory. Choosing mostly whole foods will result in better nutrient assimilation and better metabolism. This ensures that you're fueling your body for vitality, superior health and improved immune function.

Examples of whole foods: Vegetables, whole grains and starchy vegetables; healthy fats, such as avocado, nuts and olive oil; beans, legumes, and lean sustainably-raised meats.

Ask yourself, "What whole foods have I eaten today? At breakfast? At lunch?" Have you ingested a salad or piece of fruit? Was there anything green on your plate? Did you put olive oil or nuts on your salad? Did you also have a glass of water? A good rule of thumb is to work toward making 90 percent of what you're fueling your body with whole foods, leaving space for occasional fake foods. You'll notice more energy than ever when you incorporate pure water, vegetables, whole grains, and protein sources. Incorporate greens two or three times a day and watch your energy soar! Incidentally, adding greens also reduces sugar cravings.

When my clients began eating whole foods, there was additionally a dramatic drop in cellular toxicity via bioenergetic screenings. My theory: Not only were they putting less chemicals in their body, the body was free to maintain homeostasis at a higher, more efficient level too!

## A Revolutionary Practice

Studies show that how we eat is as important as what we eat. This is Mindful, Intuitive Eating.

I am suggesting that you bring the "ordinary moments" practice into mealtime that we discussed in Section II. Eat with gratitude, slowly, while sitting. Smell, taste, chew. Consciously, intuitively, mindfully! This one change transformed my habitual over-eating into eating when I needed to refuel. Slowly but surely, I effortlessly dropped the pounds I had gained over menopause. Bringing a sacred element into mealtime doesn't mean not enjoying your food, rather it leads to enjoying it more.

*NOTES*

*NOTES*

*NOTES*

# Bringing It All Together

LET'S REVIEW:

## *The Five Steps to Higher Self Care*

1. Access Your Intuition
2. Identify the Barriers
3. Dive Into the Interference
4. Let Go of the Blockages
5. Experience Authentic Joy

The way back to peace is not around but through each element.

## THOUGHT – AIR

Use this formula, one thought at a time.

**Identify** the thought and **dive into** it by examining it on paper. Is it a fact or an opinion? If not fact, **let it go** and reframe it to a thought that helps instead of hinders you.

I used to write whole pages of my inner narrative and then examine one thought at a time. I found that after practicing for a while, with just one or two sentence dissections, the entire story that was effectively interfering with my inner calm would fall away like dominos. Only the unadulterated facts remained.

## EMOTION – WATER

**Identify** the emotion and **dive into** it by experiencing whatever emotion is present now. After about 90 seconds of bringing your full attention to it with curiosity, simply **let go** and release it.

Remember to skip the story. As noted earlier, thought feeds emotion. It's important to let go of the story in our heads to effectively release emotion. You can always torture yourself with the story later. Don't be surprised if, after this exercise, the underlying thought dissolves completely and along with it, its potency too.

The act of diving into emotion eventually brings you back to the peace that was always there. Sometimes it takes more than one round.

When you allow emotion to flow, rather than bottling it up, a miraculous thing happens. Inspired thought, as well as inspired action, show up along with a sense of certainty and inner peace.

## PHYSICAL – EARTH

**Identify** the area of imbalance in your life and **dive into** it by exploring all aspects that make up your day. After you've decided which area, choose an action step that comes to mind, **let go** and rebalance it by taking that action step over the next two weeks.

Identifying where your life is out of balance and taking one small step starts a chain reaction of balance in all areas. In my experience, it serves to reevaluate your life and rebalance using this formula once or twice each month.

1. Access Your Intuition
2. Identify the Barriers
    - Is it a thought,
    - an emotion
    - or a physical imbalance?
3. Dive Into the Interference

    **The 3 E's**

    - Examine the thought
    - Experience the emotion
    - Explore the area of imbalance in your physical world
4. Let Go of the Blockages

    **The 3 R's**

    - Reframe the thought
    - Release the emotion
    - Rebalance the area of imbalance in your physical world
5. Experience Authentic Joy

The beauty of these steps is that the solution to the problems that you are currently facing are literally weaved into the problem itself. Our small mind tendency to look for peace and enlightenment in all the wrong places is actually serendipitous. When you can no longer maintain your sense of peace with accessing your higher Self through meditation, nature, exercise, music, or yoga, that's when life lessons arise. Earth school is now in session.

In frustration we choose the quick fix, the ice cream, the purchase, the glass of wine, the chips, social media, retail therapy, focusing on fixing another, escaping into over working or never-ending "to-do" lists.

Your perceived obstacles are really the stepping stones that bring you back home. Herein lies the freedom and peace that you've been seeking. It's in the "slowing down." It's in the willingness to dive into your biggest challenge.

## Self-Check List

FIRE, connecting to Source:

- Do I give myself space and time to experience that which connects me to my inner knowing?
- How do I practice accessing my higher Self, the light within that never goes out?
- Can I add in meditation, quiet reflection, silence, stillness into my day?

AIR, Barrier #1 – Thoughts:

- What am I thinking?
- How do these thoughts circulating in my head keep me stuck?
- Is negative mind chatter interfering with my feelings of worthiness, self-confidence, interpersonal relationships or sleep?

WATER, Barrier #2 – Emotions:

- How in tune am I with my emotions?
- Can I identify in a given moment what I am really feeling with curiosity?
- Can I feel the different vibrations of anger, sadness, and fear?
- What about acceptance, courage, or happiness?

- Do I have the courage to explore the fluidity of my emotions?

EARTH, Barrier #3 – Navigating the physical world that we inhabit:

- Am I willing to look at all aspects of my earthly existence?
- Is there a chronic issue regarding my career, finances, relationships, sleep, etc.?
- What are the obstacles to achieving my health goals?
- What can I do to move toward whole foods 90 percent of the time?
- How much pure water do I drink? Is it at least 64 ounces? If not, how can I increase my water intake?

Am I ready to ask for support in moving me closer to higher self-care practices? Ask for the willingness to be truly honest with yourself.

How long have I been dealing with the above issues? Is it time to ask for help?

How do I apply these steps to my life?

- Can I do this on my own?
- Where do I begin?
- What's the next step?

Now that you've gotten a taste of how to bring yourself back to center and authentic joy, how do you apply all this to your life?

You have always made ends meet, resourceful is your middle name, but to invest in yourself seems selfish and you feel on some level that you are undeserving.

Are you worth it?

I know for certain that within you already exists your road map back to peace. The love and light within you is quietly waiting to be reawakened. You have continued to read to this point because you know there has got to be a better way. You're ready and willing to do what it takes to be the best you can be from this moment forward.

Let's do it! In my vision, you are already the energetic, life-loving leader you were meant to be.

Take the next step.

Let's begin, now, to remove the barriers together!

## IN CLOSING:

"'Heaven and earth shall pass away' means that they will not continue to exist in separate states."

– *A Course in Miracles*

These days it's rare that I don't awaken with childlike glee and unfathomable joy, sometimes followed by tears of utter amazement when I realize from whence I've come on this incredible earth journey. Today, when troubled, I almost instantaneously get excited, for I know this is yet another earth lesson, and I have an unwavering Inner Guide, as well as a plethora of foolproof tools. The best part is that I have the honor of sharing this with you.

Beyond the ages, beyond time and space, you are the essence of the love and light that you seek. Your task is merely to recall this ancient knowing. You are the reason that I have offered my story. It is by extending love through these pages that I realize our oneness and the perfect innocence and love that I am too.

Seek, not for love, for that is what you are.

Delight the universe by spreading your arms wide open and receive the love that surrounds you now and forever.

This version of the Lord's prayer sums it up beautifully and has helped me to step out of guilt and into a new realm, opening fully to a gracious, joy-filled authentic life. May it serve you as well.

> Our Father, who art in heaven, hallowed be thy name. Thy Kingdom come, Thy Will be done, on earth as it is in Heaven. Give us this day our daily earth lessons that inevitably lead us back to You. And forgive us our imagined trespasses, as we forgive those who we think trespassed against us but never did in truth. And lead us not into temptation, but deliver us from ego thoughts.
>
> For Thine is the Kingdom, the Power and Glory forever and ever. Amen.

# Bibliography


Brown, M. (2005). *The Presence Process: A Healing Journey Into Present Moment Awareness.* Beaufort Books.

Byron, K. (2003). *Loving What Is: Four Questions That Can Change Your Life.* Three Rivers Press.

Chödrön, P. (2005). *Getting Unstuck: Breaking Your Habitual Patterns & Encountering Naked Reality* [Audio Book]. Sounds True, Inc.

Colgrove, M., Bloomfield, H. H., & McWilliams, P. (1976). *How to Survive the Loss of a Love.* Prelude Press.

Colquhoun, J., & ten Bosch, L. (2012). *Hungry for Change* [Film]. Permacology Productions.

David, M. (2005). *The Slow Down Diet: Eating for Pleasure, Energy and Weight Loss.* Healing Arts Press.

Dwoskin, H. (2003). *The Sedona Method: Your Key to Lasting Happiness, Success, Peace and Emotional Well-being.* Sedona Press.

Gameau, D. (2014). *That Sugar Film* [Film]. Madman Production Company.

Jampolsky, G. (1979). *Love is Letting Go of Fear.* Celestial Arts.

Lawrence, B. (1977). *The Practice of the Presence of God* (J. Delaney, Trans). Penguin Random House.

Peale, N. V. (2003). *The Power of Positive Thinking.* Weiser Books.

Schucman, H. (2008). *A Course in Miracles: Combined Volume.* Foundation for Inner Peace.

Taylor, J. B. (2009). *My Stroke of Insight: A Brain Scientist's Personal Journey.* Penguin Books.

Tolle, E. (1999). *The Power of Now: A Guide to Spiritual Enlightenment.* New World Library.

W., B. (1939) *Alcoholics Anonymous: The Big Book.* Ixia Press.

# About the Author

Donna Lee Humble, founder of bioSynergy Better Health, is an International Lifestyle & Wellness Coach and Holistic Health Practitioner, specializing in computerized bioenergetic testing. She is a Spiritual Teacher, Speaker, Emotional Release Expert, and Creator of the Higher Self Care series, leading workshops and group and private wellness programs. Since 2001, she is known around the globe for bringing you back to the wisdom within by empowering you to embrace your passion, purpose and natural state of peace in body, mind and spirit. Having overcome a plethora of emotional trauma and physical ailments herself through natural means, she has joyfully served thousands of holistic-minded women and men as they refine their health and wellness.

Donna Lee lives in the heart of the Rocky Mountains of Colorado. She finds great pleasure in traveling to the beach as often as possible. A professional wildlife watercolor artist, she enjoys painting, hiking in nature, yoga, tennis, river rafting, skiing and spending quality time with her husband, two adult children and grandchildren whenever possible.

To learn more about Donna Lee Humble and her practice, she may be contacted via:

Donna Lee Humble
812 Grand Ave., Suite 218
Glenwood Springs, CO 81601
970-274-1680
https://biosynergybetterhealth.com/

*NOTES*

# *NOTES*

*NOTES*

*NOTES*

*NOTES*

*NOTES*

*NOTES*

# *NOTES*

Made in the USA
Las Vegas, NV
14 October 2021

32264965R00118